The

bring magical results!

"Corporate bullies won't kick sand in your face after you master a few of Bill Herz's mystifying tricks from this great book."

E. James Morton
Chairman and Chief Executive Officer
John Hancock Mutual Life Insurance Company

"Astonishing is just the right word for Bill Herz's wonderful book. His techniques do indeed perform magic: They turn ordinary executives into artists who thrill and baffle."

Bert C. Roberts, Jr.
President and Chief Operating Officer
MCI Communications Corporation

"FANTASTIC! . . . Bill Herz's magical methods are easy fun to learn, are memorable, and they work wonders."

Carolyn F. Vesper
Vice President, National Circulation Sales
USA Today

"MARVELOUS AND MEMORABLE! . . . Bill Herz's magic helps punctuate a point in a way that no one ever forgets."

Walter E. (Bud) Gates
President and Chief Executive Officer
Rent-A-Center, Inc.

SECRETS
—OF THE—
ASTONISHING EXECUTIVE

BILL HERZ
WITH PAUL HARRIS

Illustrated by Lino Saffioti

AVON BOOKS ◆ NEW YORK

SECRETS OF THE ASTONISHING EXECUTIVE is an original publication of Avon Books. This work has never before appeared in book form.

AVON BOOKS
A division of
The Hearst Corporation
1350 Avenue of the Americas
New York, New York 10019

Copyright © 1991 by Bill Herz and Paul Harris
Front cover photograph courtesy of Michele Curel
Interior illustrations by Lino Saffioti
Published by arrangement with the authors
Library of Congress Catalog Card Number: 91-21040
ISBN: 0-380-76244-7

Library of Congress Cataloging in Publication Data:

Herz, Bill.
  Secrets of the astonishing executive / Bill Herz, Paul Harris.
    p. cm.
  1. Management games.   I. Harris, Paul, 1954–
HD30.26.H47   1991   91-21040
658.4'09—dc20   CIP

First Avon Books Trade Printing: November 1991

AVON TRADEMARK REG. U.S. PAT. OFF. AND IN OTHER COUNTRIES, MARCA REGISTRADA, HECHO EN U.S.A.

Printed in the U.S.A.

OPM 10 9 8 7 6 5 4 3 2 1

Acknowledgments

A great big hug and a kiss to Irene, Ellen, and Eleanor. The dot subtly wouldn't have been possible without Wyman Jones. And to Inga Boudrea for her rousing kitchen pep talk. Patti Breitman, Mark Gompertz, and Matt Keener for all the pre-book stuff. Hats off to Deb, Hazel, Francine, Rick, and, of course, Bob, who knows "everybody." And for all their guidance and support to Chuck Martinez, Eric Mead, Michael Weber, Virginia Bartee, Jim Wetherbe, Steve Solomon, Michael and Jennifer, Barbara Loomis, Patricia MacDougall, Looy, George Ort, and Bob Kohler.

Special thanks to Mac King . . . comedic genius and Fig Newton aficionado. John Kennedy . . . practical engineer of the highly improbable. Max Maven . . . developer of interactive mind games for corporate clients.

Special special thanks to Ken Turner and Paul Cummins.

And to Dana, the newest mini-amazer.

And, of course, to the entire Herz and Harris clans who have probably had enough of this stuff already . . .

. . . And to Janet and Gwenn, who deserve much more than their own page.

Preface

In 1987 Magicorp Productions was started in New York City. We formed the company to teach business leaders custom-designed tricks and illusions that they would perform to communicate their meeting objectives in an entertaining and memorable fashion.

Since that time we have worked with hundreds of companies throughout the United States, Canada, Europe, and Asia. Our clients include such companies as IBM, AT&T, Coca-Cola, Kraft General Foods, General Electric, and scores of other Fortune 500 companies as well as countless smaller corporations.

Automobile executives have made new cars magically appear to introduce a new model. Pharmaceutical execs have demonstrated the magical healing powers of their new products. Insurance execs have used illusions to demonstrate how to flatten, mangle, and shish kebab the competition.

Executives have magically appeared and disappeared in oversized versions of their product. They've illustrated their new packaging or service attributes in dazzling ways that audiences would have never expected. More than one sales exec has cut a member of his sales force in half to demonstrate you can't be in two places at one time, and many new products have shown their profitability by instantly turning into bowls of cash.

Themes of teamwork, communication, future challenges, excellence, quality, change, partnership, and numerous other business principles have all been visually demonstrated in front of large audiences through the strategic use of astonishment.

Each of these top execs realized the power of delivering a message in a nontraditional fashion. Each of these execs used magic to take away the predictability of a presentation to substantially increase its impact.

Over the years business leaders and sales execs have requested Magicorp to design illusions with business themes that can be presented one on one and for small groups. Portable briefcase-size magic that was just as astonishing as the large illusions but didn't require elaborate props or special equipment.

And thus *Secrets of the Astonishing Executive* was born. A book full of easy-to-do "mini-amazers" that you can present in the office, at lunch, during meetings, or whenever you feel the urge to be astonishing. We hope you enjoy.

Contents

Introduction

Account Executive	Mail Room Clerk	Elevator Operator	Senior VP Marketing
CFO	President	VP Sales	CEO
Up & Coming Astonishing Executive	File Clerk	Shoe Polisher	Supply Clerk

1. Move your finger **left** or **right** to the nearest **white** box
2. Move your finger **up** or **down** to the nearest **gray** box
3. Move your finger **diagonally** to the nearest **white** box
4. Move your finger **left** or **right** to the nearest **gray** box
5. Remember the job title that your finger is on, concentrate on it, and look at the next page.

Are you concentrating? Good. Now don't tell me . . . let me guess. Hmmm . . . is there a letter *E* in the job title that you're thinking of?

"Yeah but that's no big deal, a lot of the job titles have an *E*."

. . . but only one of them is surrounded with a *C* on one side and an *O* on the other.

"Wow . . . how'd you know I was thinking of CEO?"

That's nothing, I'm just warming up. Read on and I'll tell you all about it.

You're at a tense business lunch, struggling to make personal contact with a bunch of potential clients. Your guests politely nod at your chitchat. You run out of chitchat. They continue to nod politely. You sense that you're not making a profound impression. You know for a fact that you're not having a lot of fun.

So you try telling a joke. But you're not a great joke teller. Then you try striking up a conversation about the prospects' personal interests. But their personal interests aren't all that interesting.

So there you sit . . . politely nodding at one another. The awkward silence punctuated by the sound of crunched bread sticks.

What can you do to break the ice? What can you do to make these strangers interested in you and your products? And what do these pressing problems have to do with the Instant Astonishment Move Your Finger chart on page xvii?

This is what *Secrets of the Astonishing Executive* is all about. How you can create fun moments of astonishment to break the ice, get a client's attention, get your products and proposals talked about and remembered, and get *you* talked about and remembered.

Notice what just happened. We started off as complete strangers. We had nothing in common, nothing to talk about. I was just another forgettable book salesman.

But then I got you involved in that instant astonishment thing—and I got your attention. Cut through your indifference. Your natural attraction to astonishment has broken the ice.

And now I'm going to read your mind.

You're thinking you could never learn to be astonishing. You're all thumbs. You don't have hours and hours to commit to learning a new skill. And if you can't tell jokes you certainly can't be astonishing.

Well, you're about to be astonished again. Most of the astonishment in this book can be learned in two minutes or less . . . and will astonish the most critical mind. You'll be able to demonstrate your ability to make profits for your clients by turning a one into a one hundred (see page 89) or ripping up an old product brochure and restoring it to a new one (see page 140) or even making your business card part of an unforgettable business experience.

"Yeah . . . but is this . . . I hate to say it . . . is this really appropriate behavior for a respectable executive to engage in? Isn't business supposed to be serious? Don't I have an image to worry about? Shouldn't this sort of frivolity be kept separate from my business life?"

I used to think the same thing myself. My business was always strictly as a magician who performed solely at sales meetings, conventions, and corporate events. After the entertainment ended the serious business would start.

I always kept the two separate in my mind, but then an astonishing thing started to happen. After the shows, top execs would come up to me and ask if I could teach them some illusions. I thought they wanted to learn just for fun, for the sheer kick of being astonishing.

But that wasn't it. These top execs saw the astonishing potential of astonishment as a *communication tool*. These successful execs saw astonishment as a nonverbal way to get their message across, to stand out from the crowd and command attention—and to have fun in the process.

I listened to these Fortune 500 execs and realized that they were right, that the business of magic and the magic of business were one and the same. And that's when I began a new company to customize presentations and teach executives, speakers, and sales people how to use astonishment in their own presentations and to gain an interactive edge in their business relationships.

My ongoing collaboration with these exceptional execs has uncovered a wide variety of practical business uses for astonishment, including "reading a client," "dissolving tension," "breaking down barriers," "creating a window of opportunity," "commanding attention," and "humanizing managerial relationships." All of these topics and more are covered in the following pages.

How to Use This Book

Secrets of the Astonishing Executive is a collection of strategically designed "mini-amazers"—portable units of instant astonishment that you can use in a variety of business situations.

Each mini-amazer is broken down into six sections:

1. Building Blocks
2. Problem
3. Solution
4. Astonishing Secret
5. Troubleshooter
6. Memo

Building Blocks

Each mini-amazer opens with quick tips from top execs. Business building blocks that I have collected through my collaboration with real-life astonishing execs. These proven rules of thumb have laid the foundation for many successful careers.

Think about how these thoughts apply to your career, because when the ground rules are ignored, the real problems begin.

Problem

This presents a business situation that's gotten out of hand and generally looks hopeless. Think about how you'd handle the problem. Be as wild and creative in your solutions as possible. This kind of over-the-top brainstorming will often produce practical, down-to-earth solutions.

Solution

A mini-amazer comes to the rescue. By using a mini-amazer you can create a strategic moment of astonishment.

Some of the solutions can be used as practical real world business tools, while others will be appropriate in a wide range of circumstances. And I've thrown in some that are strictly for fun.

These astonishing solutions can be used to warm up a client, spice up a speech, or to simply cheer up the office gang. Exactly when and where is up to you, but you won't be able to be astonishing until you've discovered the astonishing secret.

Astonishing Secret

This is where you learn that special bit of information you need to be astonishing. It's the "how to" of the amazing part. A massive amount of R&D has gone into creating maximum astonishment for minimum effort. You can usually learn the basic secret in less than two minutes. But as in any speech or presentation, know what you're going to say or do before you say it or do it.

And in any good presentation or speech, you must find the words and gestures that fit your personality. If you're not naturally funny, don't try to be funny. The mini-amazer will create the fun part for you. Your job is to let the presentation flow naturally out of your own personality . . . as if it were an ordinary conversation. After you've done one or two you won't believe how effective and easy they are. And if you have any questions, the troubleshooter section should set you straight.

Troubleshooter

The mini-amazers are designed to be trouble-free. The troubleshooter section addresses some of your "what-ifs." The what-ifs will probably never come up but are included for your peace of mind.

Once you've presented a few mini-amazers—and have been on the receiving end of gasps of amazement and chortles of delight—you'll want to be astonishing whenever the occasion demands. In fact, sometimes you'll make the occasion demand. But anytime you get the urge to be astonishing, check the memo first.

Memo

Contains the bare bones of the secret stuff. A quick glance at the memo will refresh your memory on the key points of the secret.

By following the steps included with each mini-amazer your business life should become problem free. Okay, maybe not problem free. Yes, you'll still have those moments when you'll be let down, disappointed, frustrated, angry, used . . . you know, your basic business emotions. So now instead of wasting energy on how to get even, the next time you feel the urge to commit executive hari-kari read one of the executive bridge burners first.

Bridge Burners

These are truly twisted scams that are meant to be savored and fantasized over until you have a chance to cool off. Bridge burners are intended for your entertainment purposes. Don't ever try a bridge burner for real. There . . . I've said it . . . however, if you do, drop me a line; I'd love to hear what happened.

All right. Enough small talk. It's time to get your clients' attention. It's time to get your products and proposals talked about and remembered. It's time to get *you* talked about and remembered. It's time to have some serious fun. Lock the door. Unplug the phone. Stick your feet up on the desk . . . and prepare to become an Astonishing Exec.

1

The Soon-to-Be-Astonishing Executive

The Rapid Response Résumé

Words are cheap. What you do is what you are. If you claim that you are a cut above the rest, show them from the start.

Problem

You're trying to increase the callback rate on your résumé. So you've hired an award-winning résumé writer. He makes your high school car-washing job sound like a strategic quality control position for Lee Iacocca.

Your too-wonderful-to-be-true résumé is printed on classic-laid watermarked eggshell paper, slightly oversized to stick out from any pile, and stuffed into a crease-resistant laser-printed envelope, subtly scented to smell like freshly minted currency.

Your brilliantly conceived and executed résumé arrives on your prospective employer's desk along with eighty or ninety other slightly oversized résumés. He doesn't call. He doesn't write. Nothing.

If only you could have put something intriguing into your résumé to give you an interactive edge . . . oh well.

Solution

Your prospective employer is about to toss your résumé into the ''probably not'' pile, when something curious listed under your ''Special Interests'' catches his eye:

Mind reader . . . Call me and find out.

Hmmm . . . what the heck? It's more fun than reading eighty-seven more wonderfully written résumés, so he phones you up. You chitchat about the job, and then he

1

pops the question: What's this mind reading thing you do? We could sure use one around here. Ha ha ha. And you say, "Well, sir, to be perfectly honest, it's not actually mind reading, it's more of a psychological thing. If you're interested, we can try it over the phone right now." Who could pass up the chance to participate in a psychological mind reading thing over the phone? Of course he says yes.

While on the phone you fax your prospective employer a special chart listing various job skills. Then over the phone you direct him to make a random selection of any one of them.

Then still over the phone you read his mind by telling him the exact random job skill he selected!

The astonished prospective employer can't help but notice it is a valuable job skill that his ideal employee would possess. You casually mention that you possess that very same valuable job skill. Gee . . . what a coincidence!

The prospective employer goes back to reading the other eighty-seven wonderfully written résumés . . . but you'll be the one that he talks about and remembers.

Astonishing Secret

Yep, it's a version of Max Maven's Instant Astonishment Move Your Finger chart, which you personally customize to highlight your own job skills.

Customizing the Instant Astonishment Chart

1. Make a copy of the blank chart in Figure 1–1 (see page 5).
2. Type or print your most memorable job skill in the middle right-side square as shown in Figure 1–2.
3. Fill in the rest of the squares with your numerous secondary job skills. (See Figure 1–3 for examples.)

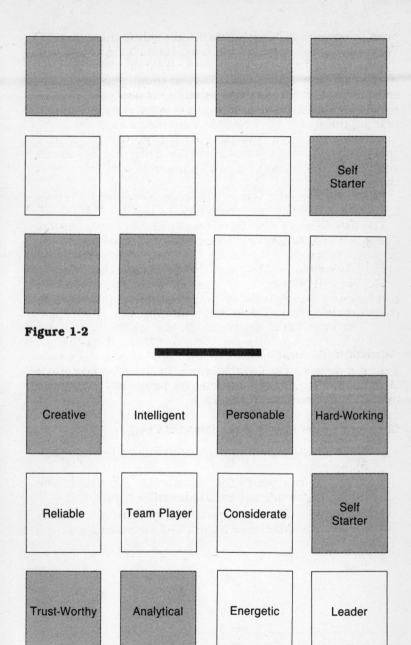

Figure 1-2

Creative	Intelligent	Personable	Hard-Working
Reliable	Team Player	Considerate	Self Starter
Trust-Worthy	Analytical	Energetic	Leader

Figure 1-3

3½

While You're on the Phone Fax a copy of your filled-in chart to your prospective employer, then give him the following instructions over the phone.

1. Place your finger on any **gray** square.
2. Move your finger **left** or **right** to the nearest **white** square.
3. Move your finger **up** or **down** to the nearest **gray** square.
4. Move your finger **diagonally** to the nearest **white** square.
5. Move your finger **left** or **right** to the nearest **gray** square.
6. Concentrate on the job skill that your finger is on.

Then You Say "By the way, did I mention that one of my strongest attributes is that I'm a *self starter*." (In place of self starter you say whatever key attribute you printed in the middle right-side square).

While on the other end of the phone, where your prospective employer's mind and finger are focused on that very same job skill, you'll hear the words, "How'd you do that?"

In your most employable problem-solver voice respond, "I'd be glad to explore that question with you . . . when we meet in person for my interview."

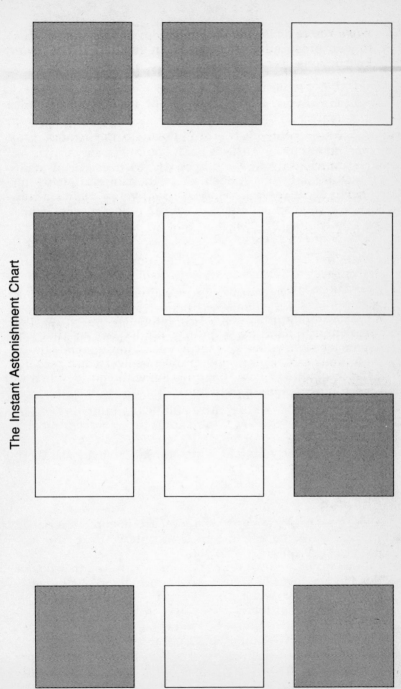

The Instant Astonishment Chart

Figure 1-1

The Forget-Me-Not
Business Card Handout #1

A successful executive anticipates the needs of the people he is dealing with. If you are in sales, anticipating objections makes for an easier sale. If you are in service (we all are), anticipating what services will be needed can make you stand out. And in business relationships, anticipating others' objectives will help you reach yours. Here's a way to show you can definitely anticipate others' needs—while accomplishing the crucial objective of unloading your own stock of business cards.

Problem

In the back of your desk drawer you've got a dusty box of 500 super deluxe embossed linen paper business cards. Five hundred little cardboard salesmen with your name and number on them—just waiting to remind the client to call you back and say, "Hey, I think you're swell—will you accept my money for something on which you can make an obscene profit?"

But you don't hand out many business cards for fear they'll be lost in the executive shuffle of hundreds of other business cards. So now you're stuck at home, staring at a silent phone, tears on your pillow, waiting for the call that never comes. So your 500 cardboard salesmen just sit there and sadly sigh, "Oh well."

Solution

Make your business cards part of an astonishing experience to create a memorable meeting, an unforgettable business card, and an unforgettable you.

You lay out a bunch of your business cards on the client's desk in the form of a giant question mark. Your name is already being imbedded in the client's mind by *sheer repetition*. The question is, Can you really give the client personalized service? I don't know. Let's find out.

The client gives you a randomly selected number—let's say fourteen. You personally count to the fourteenth card on the question mark. You personally turn your fourteenth business card over. It's the *only* card that has the *client's name* on the back . . . personally written by you.

The next time the client sees your card with his name on it, he'll remember the astonishing moment. He'll subconsciously remember personal service, and consciously pick up the phone—because he remembers you and thinks you're swell.

Astonishing Secret

It just works. I'm not sure how—it's just one of those things. Get a stack of forty business cards, follow the directions, and have fun. You can thank me later.

Before the Big Meeting Write "We work well together, George." on the blank side of one of your business cards and position it in your stack of forty so that it is the *twenty-first* card from the *top*. All the cards are printed-side up. And that's it! You're all set to amaze.

Politely, yet without being subservient, ask George to cut off and hold a small chunk of cards—*less than half*. Turn your back while he does this. Tell George to put his cards out of sight, as you deal out your *top twenty cards* printed-side up, into a giant question mark. Your first card starts the curvy part of the question mark. Your second card overlaps the first card, the third card overlaps the second card, and keep on dealing until you've silently counted nineteen cards. The twentieth card becomes the dot on the question mark (Figure 1–4). Put the rest of your cards out of the way.

Make a big deal about how there's no way a normal exec could possibly know how many cards he holds.

Have him count his cards. Let's say he has ten. Then counting out loud, using George's number, count each card, moving up the question mark. *Starting at the dot as number one*, your next card is number two, and so on, until you've counted ten cards on the question mark. Turn the number ten card over to reveal the "We work well together, George." card! The astonished client will remember you from now on—unless of course his name isn't George—in which case you might want to make the proper adjustment.

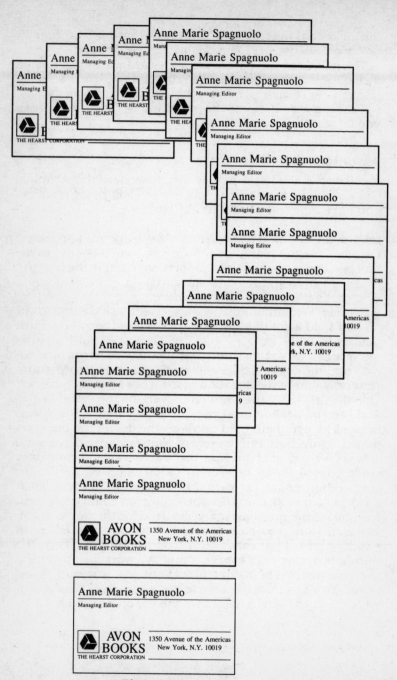

Figure 1-4

Troubleshooter

Question: Boy is my face red—I counted to the card and it wasn't there. What happened?

Answer: This is a super easy thing, *but* you've got to follow the rules: (1) The secret card must be twenty-first from the top—that means twenty cards are on *top* of the message card. (2) You dealt out twenty-one cards instead of twenty. Remember, your magic numbers are twenty-one (for the stack) and twenty (for the question mark deal). (3) You didn't count from the dot. (4) You forgot to use the client's number to count with.

MEMO

The Forget-Me-Not
Business Card Handout #1

1. Client's card is number twenty-one from the top of forty cards. All cards are printed-side up.
2. Client cuts off less than half the cards.
3. Silently count the top twenty cards into a question mark starting from the curve. The twentieth card is the dot.
4. The client counts his cards.
5. Use client's number to count up the question mark, starting at the dot. Count out loud. The card you count to will be the client's name card.
6. Rehearse a few times just before meeting the client to make extra sure you remember the sequence.

Question: What happens if I do this and the client says, "You are the most intriguing person I have ever met. I am ready to sign the contract, but before I do, could you do one more unforgettable thing with your business cards?"

Answer: You need a nifty forget-me-not variation that demonstrates your supernatural ability to anticipate a client's needs however sordid they may be.

The Forget-Me-Not
Business Card Handout Bonus

1. On the blank side of one of your business cards write "George just ran out of cards."

2. Position George's card twenty-one from the top and proceed exactly as before, stopping after the part where you've dealt out the question mark.

3. The question of the day is, Can you anticipate the client's needs? Let's find out.

4. Tell George to deal his first card onto the table. You follow by taking the dot card, turning it over, and placing it blank side up onto George's card. George deals another card onto the first two card pile. You follow by putting the next card of the question mark onto the pile.

5. Continue this back and forth dealing until George runs out of cards, then turn over the next question mark card—"George just ran out of cards."—leaving the client with an unforgettable memory of you and your business card.

GASP FACTOR

Astonishing Reactions

People's reactions to mini-amazers are a clue to how they think.

- People who aggressively want to know the secret right away tend to be interested in the *details* of a product or program.
- People who aren't especially concerned to know the secret tend to be more interested in the overall *results* of a product or program.
- People who give you a blank stare no matter what you do tend to be your teenage children.

2

The Astonishing Office

The Extra-Special Client Mind-Reading Rolodex

Nothing is more important to someone than his or her own name. Here's a way to show a client that, to you, they're not just another Joe.

Problem

An insecure client glumly stares at your industrial strength Rolodex with its 22,000 client cards. The underloved client wonders if you really care about him, or do you see him as just another pretty checkbook? You try to put his fears to rest . . . when he notices your hand caressing his checkbook's knee. The client is heartbroken. His checkbook doesn't know what to think.

You've got to do something astonishing to make your client feel extra special.

Solution

Give your client a fresh tissue, then ask him if he wants to stick his finger into your Rolodex. At first he'll be taken aback, but you convince him it won't hurt—he might even like it.

You pull out a chunk of slotted Rolodex cards and show they're filled in with different clients' names and numbers. You then flip through the cards and let him stick his finger onto *any card he wants*. The client pulls out the random Rolodex card and discovers that the card *has his name and number on it*. "'How can this miracle be?" he asks.

You shrug your shoulders. "I have no idea, but my Rolodex only does this with *extra-special clients*." The overwhelmed client breaks into song and gives you a hug . . . as you play footsie with his checkbook under the desk.

Astonishing Secret

A hunk of Rolodex cards are booby-trapped to do all the astonishing stuff for you.

Preparation—Making the Booby Trap

1. Take thirty to forty blank Rolodex cards from the office supply room, divide them in *half*. Fill in half of the cards with names and phone numbers of mythical contacts. It doesn't matter whose names or numbers are on the cards so long as the cards look normal.

2. Take the other half of the cards and fill in each one with the name and phone number of the client you want to impress. Now you have fifteen or twenty duplicates of the special client's cards.

3. Take the whole chunk of *duplicate client* cards over to a paper cutter and trim approximately ¹⁄₁₆ inch off the top of each card (Figure 2–1).

4. Clean up the mess, put a Band-Aid on your finger and look at what you've got: (a) A bunch of normal Rolodex cards filled in with various names and numbers. (b) A bunch of client duplicate Rolodex cards. This bunch is a tad shorter than the first bunch, but not enough to where anyone would notice.

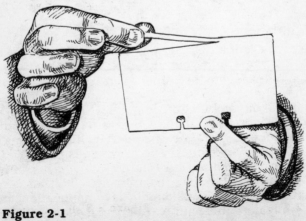

Figure 2-1

5. Combine the two batches of cards to make one big stack so that *every other card will be a short client card.* Make sure one of the nonduplicated cards is in front. After you've put the entire batch together, put all the cards in the front of the Rolodex so you can easily remove the entire batch when that extra-special someone comes to visit.

When You're Ready to Be Astonishing   Pop out the batch of booby-trapped cards. Make sure they're nice and neat, and hold them at the slotted ends *tightly* with your left fingers. Riffle the top of the cards with your right thumb—from front to back (Figure 2-2)—and a weird thing will happen.

You'll only be able to see the normal names—it's as if the duplicate client cards have disappeared. Don't be alarmed. This is exactly what you want to happen. You want the cards to look like a normal batch of names—and that's what the client sees, just a bunch of miscellaneous names and numbers. Don't make a big deal out of this. Just riffle them once or twice, and the client will be convinced that all is as it seems to be.

Slowly riffle the cards again and tell the client to stick his finger *anywhere* into the Rolodex cards as you riffle them (Figure 2–3). Let him take out the randomly fingered card

Figure 2-2   **Figure 2-3**

where he'll discover he's selected his own Rolodex card. Destiny has fingered him as an extra-special client. If the client shivers with excitement at the sight of his own name give him an extra thrill.

Extra Thrill Take the card he's holding and put it at the front of your Rolodex packet. Now by riffling the tops of the cards *from back to front* (the reverse of how you riffled before), *all* the cards will transform into cards with his name on them! When you're done riffling, pop the cards back into the Rolodex, close the lid, give your egoed-out client a moment to get over himself, then ask him to give you something nice. You never know, it's worth a shot.

Troubleshooter

Question: What if the client grabs the cards and sees all the ones with his name on them?

Answer: The client will be flattered that you took the effort to immortalize his name. Teach him how to riffle the cards so he can make the magic happen—a bonus for being your extra-special client.

MEMO

Extra-Special Client
Mind-Reading Rolodex

1. Divide a pile of thirty to forty blank Rolodex cards in half.
2. Fill in half with random names and phone numbers and half with the client's name and number.
3. Use a paper cutter to trim $\frac{1}{16}$ inch off the tops of all the duplicate client cards.
4. Combine the two halves so that every other card is a duplicate client card and put them in the front of your Rolodex. Be sure a nonduplicate is at the front of the stack.
5. Remove the prepared hunk of Rolodex cards and show they are normal by riffling them with your thumb from front to back.
6. Riffle again—but slowly—so the client can put his finger on a freely selected card.
7. Let the client discover he's fingered his own card.
8. *Optional:* Put client's card at face of stack and riffle the cards from *back to front* to turn them all into client's cards.
9. Send his checkbook a dozen long-stemmed roses.

The Anytime Anywhere Legendary Book Baffler

In the office, you are known by the company you keep. It's not often you see the V.P. of finance hanging out with the mail room clerk, or the director of marketing partying with the security guard. No one said business was pretty, but that's how the game is played.

And although you are judged by the company you keep, it's even more important to stand out among your associates, to be someone special in an interesting, acceptable way.

Unfortunately it is often difficult to stand out among a group of competent, eager co-workers. So here's a mini-amazer strategically designed to get the rumor mill rolling that an astonishing exec is in their midst.

Problem

You're efficient. You get the job done. You have a lap-top computer. But you're not legendary. You just don't have the clout to close the mega-dollar deals yet. Trapped in the twilight zone of semi-success you are looking for a way out. Post-its have already been invented. So what's left?

Solution

You have no choice. You're forced to reveal your secret ability to zero in on their unspoken thoughts.

Astonishing Secret

Boldness, guts, and bluff: basic tools for executive survival.

When no one's looking, take a secret glance at any normal book, around the middle of the book. Let's say page 68. Remember the last word on that page . . . let's say it's the word *gullible*. Burn "gullible, page 68" into your memory.

Now take a secret glance at a *different* normal book—at page 68—and remember the *last* word on that page . . . let's say it's the word *chowderhead*. Remember that word, too. So now in your mental storage space is "gullible chowderhead, page 68." That's it. That's all you have to remember. Don't worry about which word came from which book. Just remember the page number and the two words.

Put the two secret books on top of the book stack, at eye level on the bookshelf or some other easily accessible spot.

Doing It Tell someone to hand you a couple of books as you casually gesture toward your two secret books. Most of the time he'll grab your two secret books, which is what you want him to do.

If one or both of the two chosen books aren't your secret books, then keep asking for more and more books until your two secret books end up in the pile. Then you say, "Great, I think you've chosen a good selection here. Why don't you pick up those two?" Of course, the two books you point to are your two secret books.

What's Happened So Far? Someone's selected two random books that "you've never ever seen before in your life," but because you live right you just happen to know the last word on page 68 of both books.

The Gutsy Part Have your book person give you *one* of the two random books. He keeps the other book in his hand.

Casually riffle the pages of your book, looking away from the book, as you ask someone to say, "Stop" (Figure 2–4). Open the book at the stopped-at page. Glance at the page

Figure 2-4

number, and no matter what page number you see, *say* "Sixty-eight," then close the book, toss it aside, and say, "Turn to page 68 in your book."

Note   Try to time your riffle so that you are stopped somewhere near the middle of the book. This sounds like a tall order but is almost automatic after rehearsing it a few times with a loved one, plus you have a *lot of leeway*. You can be off by as much as one-third and still get away with the bluff. Ignore your guilt.

The Bluff Attitude . . .   is complete disinterest. It is used constantly by all astonishing execs. Pretend that selecting a random page number is a boring yet necessary part of the procedure—like another bill to be signed. You do it, toss it aside, and never think about it again. Practice doing it for real. Riffle a book and have someone say stop. Look at the page number and say it out loud. It's an uninteresting procedure at best. Notice that no one questions if you're really stopped on that page or not. So when you call out the *bluff* page number—if you keep the same matter-of-fact attitude—*everyone* will believe you stopped at whatever page you said you stopped at, which in this case is page 68.

The Key Bluff Line After Someone Stops You at a Random Page   You say "Sixty-eight . . . turn to page sixty-eight in your book."

Turn away so there's no way you could possibly get a peek at the other book, then tell the book holder to *find the last word on his chosen page, remember it, then close the book.*

The person thinking of the word will be absolutely secure in his knowledge that no one could know the word he's thinking of. A random word . . . selected from a random page . . . selected from a random book.

But you know differently. You know he's thinking of one of two words: *gullible* or *chowderhead.* You are way ahead of him. Pretend to concentrate, then ask "Is there a letter G in the word your thinking of? If there is, you know the word's *gullible.* If there isn't, you know the word's *chowderhead.**

Note of interest: The word *chowderhead* is now included in all English language dictionaries.

Whenever you feel like it, announce the word he's thinking of. Act as if it's no big deal, then stroll back to your desk. He'll never question your remarkable powers again.

Troubleshooter

Question: What if no one believes it when I bluff the page number?

Answer: This is a solid gold worry-free bluff—everyone will buy it, so long as you treat it as "a boring detail that has to be disposed of." Go out right now and try it for someone and find out that you were born to be a champion page bluffer.

Question: What if I am in someone else's office, can I still do it?

Answer: Sure. As soon as the person you are visiting leaves the office for a minute take a quick look at any two books on his or her shelf, then proceed as if you were in your own office.

MEMO

Anytime Anywhere
Legendary Book Baffler

1. When no one is looking open two books to the same page (somewhere near the middle) and remember the last word of that page in both books. So in your head is "gullible, chowderhead, page 68."

2. Put the two secret books somewhere easy to find.

3. Ask someone to get you a couple of books. If they give you the two secret books you're set. If not, just keep asking for more books so you can have a "more random selection," until the two secret books are tossed onto the pile of other books. Direct someone to pick up the two secret books, and you're set.

4. Have the book holder give you either one of his two books. You casually riffle your book, looking away from the book, until someone says stop. Try to time the riffle so you're stopped near the center of the book.

5. Glance at the stopped page and say "Sixty-eight . . . turn to page sixty-eight in your book." Casually toss your book aside, then turn away from the book holder so he knows you're not peeking.

6. Tell the book holder to remember the last word on page 68, then to close the book and concentrate on the word.

7. You know he is thinking of one of your two secretly remembered words. Pretend you're a psychic and ask if the first letter is a *G* (or whatever the first letter of one of your words is).

8. Whatever the answer, you'll know the word he's thinking of. Build up the suspense, then read his mind.

9. You've got guts; you're on your way!

The Instant Incompetency I.Q. Test

The person who gives the best interview might not be the best person for the job. You've got to get past the slick paint job and check under the hood.

But turning down seemingly qualified candidates requires a certain amount of diplomacy.

Problem

You're interviewing for office help—looking for the perfect combination of intelligence, personal hygiene, and hero worship.

Company policy requires you to tell each serious candidate why you didn't hire him or her. So far it's been easy. One person gave you a résumé on the back of a dot-to-dot coloring book. Reason for not hiring: Connected the wrong dots.

Next, a tattooed lady wearing a live python around her neck. Reason for not hiring: Python only typed thirty words a minute.

Next, Skippy, the boss's nephew. He's still learning how to spell MBA. Not only is he driving with one wheel in the sand, but he looks a lot like your cousin Eugene—the same cousin Eugene that conned you into eating a worm when you were eight years old by telling you it was organic sushi. You hate Eugene, you hate sushi, and you don't want to hire this guy. In fact, the boss doesn't want you to hire him either. But the boss promised his sister that he'd give the little goof a fair shot.

Your creativity is stretched to the max as you search for an honorable excuse to skip Skippy.

Solution

Let the inappropriate candidate disqualify himself by taking an impossible to pass I.Q. test. Tell Skippy that he's perfect for the job, but before you can formally hire him he's required to take the basic company I.Q. test. It's so simple a doorknob could pass this test. *No one in recorded history has ever failed this company I.Q. test.* It's just a dumb formality, to test Skippy's ability to follow simple directions.

You each hold a stack of five facedown business cards.

You turn one over, Skippy turns one over. You put one card on the bottom, Skippy puts one card on the bottom. You turn over another card, he turns over another card. Yes, it would take years of intensive moron training to mess up this test.

You spread out your five cards. They're all faceup. Skippy spreads out his five cards—four are faceup, one is *facedown*. "Gee that's *never* happened before. Hey, no big deal. You're the boss's nephew, we'll give you another chance." And give him the same simple test again.

Skippy's twenty years of higher education are focused with laserlike intensity on the act of turning over a business card. At the end of round two you spread your cards—of course they're all faceup. Skippy spreads his five cards, they're all faceup, except for *one facedown card*. Astonishingly, he's blown it again! You can't believe it yourself. This has never happened before. No one has ever failed the test—no one. But you really want to be fair, so you give him an even easier version of the same stupid simple I.Q. test—and the poor goof blows it again!

You give a sympathetic handshake, and carefully show him how to operate the doorknob so he can leave your office.

Reason for not hiring: Inability to follow directions . . . is the boss's nephew . . . looks like cousin Eugene.

Astonishing Secret

The only way it's possible to end up with all five cards facing the same way is if one of the cards is a special double-sided business card.

Get Ready Grab eleven business cards and a bottle of rubber cement. Carefully glue two of the cards together so the *printing* is on the *outside*. Clean off any excess glue so it looks like a normal printed business card when viewed from either side. You'll now have nine normal cards and one double-sided business card.

Before You Start Stack *all* ten cards *printed side up* so that the double card is number *seven* from the top (six cards are on top of the double card, three cards are below the double card). Put the ten cards in your pocket or on your desk before you begin the interview.

Test 1: Pick up the stack of ten cards—printed sides up—and count off the top five cards for the interviewee. Your double card should now be your *second* card from the top. Tell the interviewee that his job is to copy everything you do.

1. Spread the five cards in your hands—to show all the cards printed side up—then square the cards into a neat pack. (Be careful not to show the other side of the cards.)
2. Turn the *top* card over (the blank side is up) and place it on the *bottom* of your stack. Your alert anxious interviewee should be following along with his cards—doing exactly the same thing.
3. Take off the new top card, and place it on the *bottom* of the stack but *don't* turn it over.
4. Turn the *top* card over—place it on the *bottom* of your stack.
5. Take off the *top* card—place it on the *bottom* without turning it over.
6. Turn the top card over *on top* of the stack.
7. Turn the *entire stack* over.
8. Turn the top card over on top of the stack.
9. Spread your cards to show all five are printed side up. When the forlorn interviewee spreads his cards one will be reversed. Too bad.

Test 2: Put your *top* card on the *bottom,* and you'll be all set to give the poor guy one more chance. Let him turn his reversed card over, then repeat steps 1 through 9. He'll blow it again with one upside-down card. Gee . . . tough break.

Put your *top* card on the *bottom,* and give him one final chance to pass the test.

Test 3: Do steps 1 through 5, then spread your cards to show two reversed cards. The interviewee spreads his cards to show two reversed cards also. So far he's right on the money—the rest is cake.

Square your cards and continue with steps 6 through 9. He screwed up again. Act a little embarrassed, shake his hand, and gently suggest he pursue a less demanding career. Don't move until the wave of guilt subsides, then have a donut.

Rehearsal Tip Run through the sequence about ten times with cards in hand to make sure you remember it.

No Rehearsal Option If you don't want to remember the sequence, copy the next page and read the instructions aloud right off the "Official Employee I.Q. Test" as you administer the test to the interviewee.

The Official Employee I.Q. Test

Set up ten business cards printed side up—the double-sided card is number seven from the top. Give the top five cards to interviewee, leaving you with the double-sided card second from the top.

The Test Interviewee copies your actions.

1. Spread five cards to show all are printed side up—then square cards.
2. Turn top card *over* and place on bottom.
3. Put top card on bottom, *don't* turn it over.
4. Turn top card *over* and place at bottom.
5. Put top card on bottom, *don't* turn it over.
6. Turn top card over on *top* of stack.
7. Turn over *entire stack*.
8. Turn top card over on top of stack.
9. Spread the cards to show all five are printed side up—interviewee will have one card reversed, "whoops."

To Repeat Place your *top card on the bottom*—then follow steps 1 through 9.

Last Chance Repeat 1 through 5. You both spread to reveal two reversed cards. Square cards.

Complete steps 6 through 9 . . . the interview is over.

Have a donut.

Troubleshooter

Question: Sometimes one of *my* cards ends up reversed. Any suggestions?

Answer: You really don't want me to answer that.

The Tough-As-Nails Exercise Initiator

Sound body, sound mind. Oh, you forgot the part about the body. Whoever heard of a CEO who canceled his golf game because he was too busy? Exercise reduces stress and helps you focus when you need to concentrate.

Here's a way to avoid the stress of being the only out-of-shape body in the office by creating the illusion of being in miraculously good shape. And the oohs and aahs of admiration should then motivate you to become a genuine exercised exec.

Problem

You sit in your cubicle and attempt some office aerobics with your swivel chair. You swivel to the left. You swivel to the right. You stand up, sit down, fight fight fight. You chuckle at your little jest—and collapse into your chair from a pulled groin muscle. So there you slump and fantasize about an astonishing display of brute strength.

Solution

You warm up by mangling a few obstinate paper clips with your bare hands. Those paper clips will never play the piano again. You take a swig of Gatorade from your official Arnold Schwarzenegger thermos, then reach into your paper clip dispenser and dig out two solid steel nails. These are not wimpy wire thin nails or plastic novelty nails to amuse small children—no siree, Bob—these are genuine case hardened, reinforced steel, pound-them-in-the-wall nails.

Then with your *bare fingers* you slowly squeeze the two nails in half! Not one exec in the crowd has the muscle power to unbend what you've just bent. You casually flex your finger, and try to ignore the multiple squeaks of admiration as you go back to your work confident that they'll never kick Styrofoam peanuts in your face again.

Astonishing Secret

The two straight nails you've bent only appear to be straight. The fact is, you camouflaged two already bent nails so they appeared straight. "Is that possible?" Well, let's find out. . . .

Figure 2-5

Before You Start Clamp two nails in a vice and whack them with a hammer until you've got two U-shaped nails as in Figure 2–5. If you don't have access to a vice go to your local hardware store and talk one of the clerks into bending a couple of nails for you. Next, put the two bent nails into an empty paper clip container or other desk organizer oddity, then dump in a bunch of normal straight nails to hide the bent nails.

Being Intimidating Reach into the nail dispenser and pull out a few straight nails and hold them as shown in Figure 2–6. Look them over, then toss them back in and say "Too easy." In professional circles this is known as the "straight nail convincer." Don't worry about it.

Poke around some more and get hold of the two bent nails, and *before* you bring them out pinch them between your thumb and forefinger as in Figure 2–7. *Now* bring out the two "straight" nails.

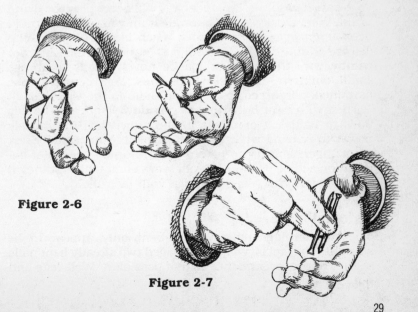

Figure 2-6

Figure 2-7

They'll look as straight as the straight nails you brought out the first time, but will be secretly bent. Now is not the time to mention this interesting fact.

The Big Bend Gently press your other thumb and first two fingers against the top and bottoms of the two nails (Figure 2–8). Flex your fingers, acting as though you are *trying* to bend the nails. If you can arrange for a bead of sweat to fall off your face and drip onto the desk blotter, all the better. Build up the suspense, then slowly "bend" the two nails (Figure 2–9). Make sure to keep the *real* bend covered.

Don't "bend" them too far—just enough to make a visible dent—then close your other hand over both nails and give them a final squeeze (Figure 2–10). The two bent nails are now loose in your fist.

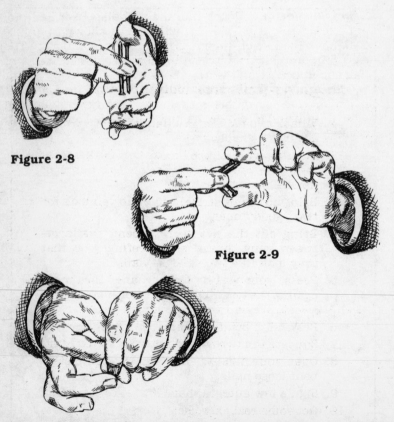

Figure 2-8

Figure 2-9

Figure 2-10

Open your hand to show the two bent nails. Let an enthralled onlooker feel the ripples in your fingers. Sign a few autographs, then go back to work.

Troubleshooter

Question: What if I drop the two nails before I finish bending them?

Answer: Act like you did it on purpose—the nails were straight, now they're bent—they'll still think you're a brute.

Question: What if I poke myself with one of the nails?

Answer: Don't do that.

MEMO

Tough-As-Nails Exercise Initiator

1. Whack two nails with a hammer until you've got two U-shaped nails.
2. Put the two U-shaped nails in a desk organizer or on your abalone shell with a bunch of normal straight nails.
3. Bring out a few straight nails as you look for two "good" ones.
4. Bring out the two secret "bent" nails between your thumb and forefinger so that they look like two straight nails.
5. Press your *other* thumb and forefinger against the two nail tops and bottoms. Grunt, sweat, pretend you're Arnold.
6. Pretend to bend the nails by flexing them.
7. Squeeze the two semi-bent nails in your fist.
8. Open your hand to show the two completely bent loose nails.
9. Sign a few autographs.
10. Get some real exercise.

The Do-It-Yourself High-Tech Exec

Technology has changed the world. Communication can now be handled efficiently, effectively, quickly, crisply, automatically, and concisely. There is only one "ly" missing. Personal*ly*. Nothing is remembered or appreciated more than delivering your message personally.

Sometimes the human factor gets lost in the high-tech shuffle. Here's a way to integrate the use of high-tech hardware with personal homemade astonishment.

Problem

You're not on the cutting edge of office technology. You're the only guy who still has a gas-powered fax with a pull cord starter. It's pretty embarrassing—all around you, whizbang execs are whizzing and banging with the latest quadralux megawhopper desktop satellite stations, while you're still getting the hang of double-stick tape. You yank the pull cord on the old fax . . . putt . . . putt . . . sputter. . . . You check the spark plugs, change the oil, and wistfully wish just once you could out-tech the high-tech exec.

Solution

Next time a techno-exec kicks into techno-talk mode, ask for his feeling about the new RX 22 phantom fax modem. "Is it worth the extra six grand or not?" When he stutters that he hasn't had a chance to check this one out yet, give him just a hint of a condescending look, then escort him into your office for a demo of your new RX 22 phantom fax modem.

You show him your fax machine. It looks like any other fax except a RX 22 modem has been installed "Where you can't see it. Of course the hot feature is the biofeedback pre-printer." Of course.

To demonstrate its amazing capabilities you give the techno-exec a newspaper and a felt-tip marker. Instruct him to hold the newspaper and marker behind his back, where he is to draw a quarter-size circle somewhere in the middle of the newspaper.

No one—not you, not him, not the RX 22 phantom fax—could possibly see where the circle is. He draws the secret circle on the newspaper, and a second later the RX 22 phantom fax spits out a square of photo-copied newspaper with a quarter-size circle around some words.

And guess what? The circled words on the faxed newspaper are the exact same words circled on the real newspaper! That's right—the RX 22 phantom fax has successfully read the techno-exec's mind! The exec will be humbled if not completely unraveled. Guide him out your door and give him some double-stick tape to play with.

Astonishing Secret

Take a folded newspaper and grab a felt-tip marker. Put them both behind your back, and without looking *draw a quarter-size circle near the middle of the paper* (Figure 2–11). Now take a look at your circle. If it's kind of lumpy and off center you did it exactly right. This is your official phantom fax prediction.

Make a copy of the circled section of newspaper. Give the photocopy prediction to a friend with a fax in another office and tell him to fax it to you when you phone with the magic words "Send me the phantom fax."

Figure 2-11

The Secret Tip   You've left the cap off your felt-tip marker so it's all dried up and won't write anymore. Basically, you want to end up with a marker that won't mark. Put the cap back on the dried marker, fold the circled newspaper page back around the rest of the newspaper, and read the funnies until the techno-exec wanders into your trap.

Doing It   Tell your pal about your new RX 22 phantom fax modem—the cutting edge of the cutting edge of high tech. Then in front of your pal, call your fax friend and say, "Send me the phantom fax." If your pal asks who you called, mumble, "I'm not allowed to reveal that and it's not important anyway." Hang up, then grab a "random felt-tip marker," which just happens to be the dry one, and a random newspaper, which just happens to be the one with the secret circle (careful to keep the circled side concealed).

Uncap the pen and give it to him to hold *behind* his back, then put the folded newspaper in his *other* hand, which he puts behind his back. Tell him to make a quarter-sized circle somewhere near the center of the paper—*without looking*. Then as soon as he's made the secret circle he's to drop the circled newspaper on the floor behind him. When the circled newspaper drops, take back the pen, recap it, then wait for the phantom fax to arrive. Let your befuddled techno-exec try to figure out why his circled section on the newspaper on the floor exactly matches the circled ad from the phantom fax.

Troubleshooter

Question: What if the circle he thinks he drew is different from my secret circle?

Answer: First, you tell him to draw a "quarter-sized" circle. This keeps the relative size within control. But even more reassuring is that it's about impossible to gage what and where you are drawing behind your back.

Question: How do I make sure the techno-exec circles the precircled side of the newspaper?

Answer: It doesn't matter which side he circles, because when he drops the newspaper to the floor he'll have no way of knowing which side was which.

MEMO

High-Tech Exec

1. Use a felt-tip marker to draw a sloppy quarter-sized circle near the center of a newspaper sheet.
2. Copy the center of the circled sheet and give to a fax friend, to be faxed to your office upon request. Replace the original circled sheet around the rest of the newspaper.
3. Leave the cap off your felt-tip marker so it dries out and becomes useless for normal marking purposes, then replace the cap.
4. When your techno buddy walks in, talk about your new "phantom fax" and phone your fax friend for delivery. Give your techno-exec the dry pen and the secretly circled newspaper behind his back (keeping the circle hidden).
5. Tell him to mark a quarter-sized circle near the center of the paper and to drop the paper on the floor.
6. Retrieve the pen, recap it, place it in your pocket.
7. Wait for the phantom fax to arrive, and let the techno-exec discover the astonishing facsimile of his circled section on the phantom fax document.

The Anti-Stress Thread Plucker

Tension in the office can quickly lead to periods of unproductiveness. A lot gets done while nothing gets accomplished. Take your work seriously, but not yourself. Here is something to help unravel the gang when they get wound a little too tight.

Problem

It's another happy-go-lucky day at the office. You're hanging around your cubicle, using scotch tape to pick cat lint off your jacket . . . when a nearby cubicle dweller notices a single strand of thread sticking from your lapel. She plucks the loose thread off your jacket . . . you're not expecting much of a thrill . . . when she notices the plucked thread is still coming out of the jacket! She pulls and pulls and pulls, and ends up with six yards of thread. Yikes! Has she destroyed the jacket and humiliated all concerned? Heck no! It was just a care-free mini-amuser to make the cubicle crowd smile.

Astonishing Secret

Drop a spool of contrasting colored thread into your inside jacket pocket. Use a needle to poke one end of the thread through to the outside of your jacket. And wait to be plucked. No one can leave a loose thread alone.

Advanced Plucker Technique As the plucked thread is pulled, hike up part of your jacket or blouse so it looks like a major seam has been unraveled. With a little acting you can get a collection started to buy you a new wardrobe.

The Astonish-Yourself Perfect-Ten Paper Clip Paradox

If you hit a wall when you're trying to solve a problem, step back and take a breather. That mental space releases the pressure and opens up your mind for other ideas.

You can create this mental space for others by giving them a moment of astonishment—there's even a way of astonishing yourself.

Problem

Your legend as an astonishing exec is growing. Your proposals are talked about and remembered. *You're* being talked about and remembered. The gasps of amazement and "hey wows" warm the cockles of your heart. But every now and then you sit by yourself alone with your warm cockles and wish that just once you could somehow astonish yourself.

Solution

Get out a bunch of paper clips, toothpicks, matches, Tums, Life Savers, coins, *anything* you have a bunch of. *Note:* A bunch is forty or more. I'll pretend you're using a bunch of paper clips so I won't get confused.

To Astonish Yourself Clear off your desk or a table and lay out a square of paper clips as shown in Figure 2–12. Put

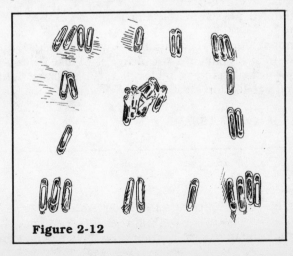

Figure 2-12

the extra clips in a pile in the middle. Doublecheck your square of paper clips with the picture to make sure you have the correct number of clips in each spot.

Your square is a perfect ten on all sides. Let's count them just for fun.

Counting the Clips Count the clips in the top row. You'll have ten clips. Count the clips on the right side—ten clips. Count the clips on the bottom row—ten clips. Count the clips on the left side row—ten clips. You can start counting from any corner up, down, or sideways, and you'll always count ten clips in each row.

Pick up a *single clip* from your extra clip pile. Hold it, feel it, kiss it good-bye, and put the clip onto the right side row as shown in Figure 2–13.

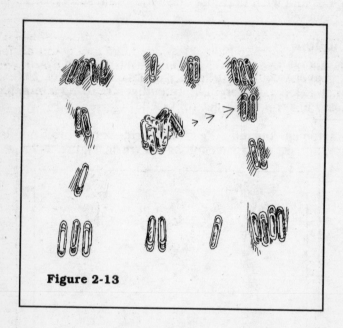

Figure 2-13

Now, move *one* clip from the *lower right corner* to a middle spot on the bottom row (Figure 2–14). You know in your heart that one of the rows must now have eleven clips.

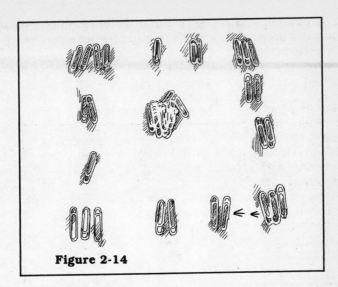

Figure 2-14

Now for the Astonishing Part One clip has vanished! I know—it's hard to believe, so go ahead and count all four rows of the square . . . and you'll still have *ten clips in each row*, even though you just added one!

Let's do it again. Take another clip from your extra pile—kiss it good-bye, and put it in the top row (Figure 2-15).

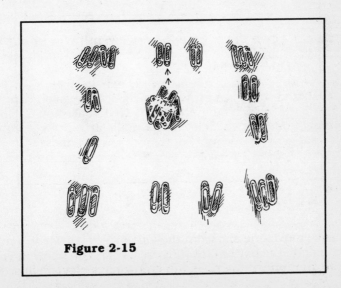

Figure 2-15

Now move one clip from the upper left corner to the left side as shown in Figure 2–16. Your logical mind insists that there has to be a row of eleven clips somewhere—so go ahead and count the four rows: ten, ten, ten, ten. Another perfect ten. "Where does the extra clip go?" I'm not prepared to answer that question.

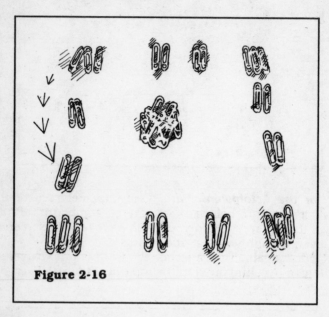

Figure 2-16

Let's Do It Again   Pick up another eleventh clip from the slush pile. Kiss it good-bye, and put it in the upper right corner as shown in Figure 2–17.

Move two clips from the same corner—one goes in the top row, and one goes on the right side row as shown in Figure 2–18. Now you know darn well that moving the position of one or two clips cannot make an extra eleventh clip disappear. So count the four rows—ten, ten, ten, ten—yikes! Okay. I give up—where does the darn clip go?

Astonishing Secret

Obviously someone's sneaking that extra clip off the table when you're not looking.

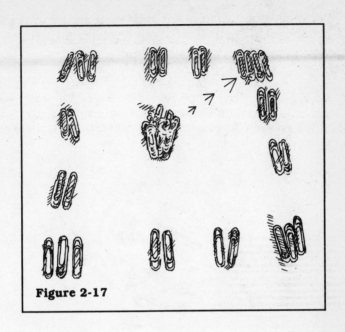

Figure 2-17

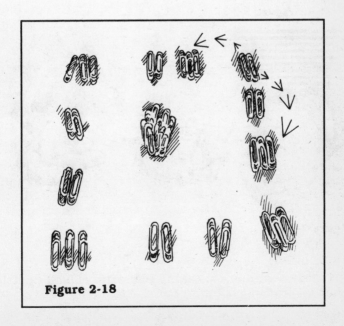

Figure 2-18

Paper Clip Paradox #2 Clip one paper clip to a folded $10 bill as shown in Figure 2-19. Fold the unclipped end of the bill back to form a "z" shape, and put a second paper clip on the bill as shown in Figure 2–20. Hold the two loose ends of the bill as shown in Figure 2–20. Pull the two ends of the bill apart and the two clips will slide together—then pop off the bill—linked in a somewhat entertaining fashion. All right, enough fooling around; pretend to go back to work.

Figure 2-19

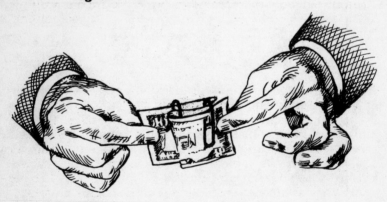

Figure 2-20

At business lunches, people become more ....ndly, more receptive, and frequently reveal their true colors. One leisurely lunch can generate the goodwill that will bring you closer to a deal than lengthy custom-designed proposals or detailed product presentations.

So when in doubt, invite someone to lunch—or better yet, find an ingenious way to get someone to invite you.

Problem

You can't understand why no one has invited you to a power lunch. You're not exactly sure what a power lunch is but you suspect it's something neat. You sadly remove your official executive lunch bib, despondently clunk your head on your desk, and find yourself staring at your business card holder. Your gurgling lunchless tummy inspires you to say, "Hmm . . . if only there was some way to hand out multiple business cards *and* get invited to lunch at the same time, but, no, that would be asking for too much."

Solution

You hand a stack of your cardboard namesakes to the potential power luncher. Direct him to deal out as many cards as he wants, then to deal that stack into two piles. There is no way a nonastonishing exec could predict which two cards would end up on top of the two stacks . . . and yet . . . when the two top cards are turned over they are inscribed with your surprise message (Figure 2–21). The potential power luncher is so astonished he has to say yes.

Figure 2-21

shing Secret

paration: Write "Let's have" on the back of one card and lunch Tuesday" on the back of another card. Put the two message cards on top of the stack of twenty or more cards.

All the cards should be printed side up.

Doing It Bring out the stack, printed side up, give it to the client, and tell him to deal the cards on the table *printed side up, one on top of the other* (Figure 2–22), and to stop dealing whenever he wants. When the client stops dealing, take the rest of the undealt cards and put them away.

Tell him to make the dealt pile nice and neat, then to pick up the dealt cards and deal them back and forth into two alternate piles, going back and forth, back and forth until he runs out of cards.

The Big Buildup Remind the client that he decided how many cards to deal. That he personally divided them into two stacks. That he had complete control over the entire situation. Tell him to turn over the top card of each stack to reveal the astonishing lunch invite.

Figure 2-22

44

Troubleshooter

Question: What if the client accidentally turns the first card over and sees the message "Let's have"— he'll think I'm sort of strange.

Answer: This is true. You must make it crystal clear that the cards are to be dealt *printed side up, before* you hand him the cards. I always deal the top two cards onto the table myself to demonstrate the procedure. I then replace the two cards on the stack, *then* give him the cards to deal himself.

Question: What if he stops dealing on the first two cards?

Answer: Don't tell him he can stop until *after* he's dealt the first two cards.

Question: What if the message card comes up backward and reads "lunch Tuesday" "Let's have," or worse, it's upside down?

Answer: Say "Hmm . . . looks like a secret message . . . I wonder what it means?" Let the client figure it out and when he says, "Let's have lunch Tuesday." Say, "I'd be delighted."

MEMO

Let's Have Lunch
Business Card Handout #2

1. Secretly write "Let's have" and "lunch Tuesday" on the blank sides of two business cards. Put them both, message side down, on top of a stack of twenty or more *printed side up* cards.
2. Give the stack to the client and have him deal the cards *printed side up*, one on top of the other, until he feels like stopping.
3. Have client pick up dealt stack and redeal it into two separate stacks, alternating back and forth.
4. The big buildup: Remind the client that he's had complete control over all the dealing—no one could know which cards would be chosen. Tell him to turn over the top card of each stack to reveal the mystery message.
5. Hose off your lunch bib.

GASP FACTOR

Focus Attention

You must focus attention before you can be understood. Presenting a mini-amazer with a business theme is an automatic attention getter that helps others focus on the issues at hand.

3

The Astonishing Lunch

The Late-for-Lunch Miracle Maneuver

We all think in terms of the big picture. But it is the lack of attention to detail that frequently causes problems, creates ill will, and builds up resentment. Like not delivering something that's promised or not returning a phone call or even being late for appointments.

These "minor" inconveniences send a clear message to your clients about your overall competence.

Clients care about results, not excuses. But when you *have* to make an excuse, make it a memorable one.

Problem

You're a tad late for your lunch meeting. You hope against hope that your client is late, too. But there he is at the table, stubble of growth on his chin, surrounded by fourteen empty nacho baskets—a haunted look in his eyes and a thin layer of dust on his briefcase. He sees you—it's too late to run. The client stands up, brushes flecks of nacho chips off his suit, and says "Okay Mr. Astonishing Exec, you better have a good excuse."

Solution

Put on your very best puppy-dog face and say, "I am really, really sorry—I was showing another client a weird psychic thing with my watch and I forgot to reset the time." The client is torn—he wants to leave and never see your puppy-dog face again. But he just has to ask, "What weird psychic thing?"

Direct your client to call over the waiter, host, or hostess of his choice. You wrap your watch in a napkin, hand it to the waiter, and tell him to go across the room, out of your sight, and secretly set the watch at any time he desires, wrap it back up in the napkin, and bring it back to you. The waiter, although leery of weird psychic things, will oblige because it's his job.

Borrow the client's watch. Pause for a moment to receive weird psychic vibrations, then set the client's watch to 6:42. The waiter arrives with napkin-wrapped watch and hands it to the client. He unwraps the watch—it's been set by the waiter to 6:42!

The client is flabbergasted—he forgets about you being late. He is so intrigued by your talents that he arrives late for his next meeting because he forgot to reset his watch. But now he has the perfect excuse, and proceeds to tell about his lunch with a truly remarkable executive.

Astonishing Secret

Two special pieces of paper hidden inside the napkin create a psychic link between you and the waiter. The first piece of paper is a $5.00 bill. The second piece of paper is a note from you.

Please help me trick my friend. Set the watch to 6:42, put it back in the napkin, and keep the money for yourself. Please destroy this note and thanks for keeping a secret.

Before You Start   When you sit down at the table put a napkin on your lap. On top of the napkin casually and without your client seeing it, place a folded $5.00 bill and the scrap of paper with the secret message (Figure 3–1). You're all set.

Take off your watch, place it on your lap, and wrap it in the napkin with the two secret papers. (The client merely sees you place the watch on your lap and wrap it up. He doesn't know that there are other secret things down there.)

Give the bundle to the waiter and tell him to go out of sight so that he can pick up the indirect gamma psychic rays. While the waiter is gone pretend to concentrate for a moment, then openly set the client's watch to 6:42.

When the waiter gets back have him hand the bundled watch directly to the client and let the client unwrap the napkin and take out the watch. Show him what time you set his watch to. They are exactly the same!

Figure 3-1

Troubleshooter

Question: What if the waiter permanently leaves with my watch?

Answer: You'll have an even better excuse next time you're late for an appointment.

Question: What if I am in an ethnic restaurant and none of the waiters speak English?

Answer: No problem. See the next page.

Spanish

Por favor ayúdame engañar a mi amigo. Pon la hora del reloj a las 6:42, vuélvalo dentro de la servilleta, y guarda el dinero. Por favor, destruye esta nota y gracias por haber guardado el secreto.

Italian

Per favore auitami a fare un scherzo a mi'amico. Fissa l'orologio per le sei e quarantadue, rimettilo in dietro in un tovagliolo e tieniti i soldi. Per favore, distruggi questa carta e grazie per mantenere il secreto.

French

S'il vous plaît, aidez-moi à tromper mon ami. Reglez là montre sur 6 heures 42, remettez dans la serviette et gardez l'argent pour vous. S'il vous plaît, detruisez cette note et merci pour garder le secret.

Japanese

どうぞ、私の友人をトリックにかけるのを、お手伝い下さい。時計を６時４２分にあわせ、それをナプキンの後ろに置いて下さい。お金は、ご自分でお持ちください。そして、どうぞ、このメモは破り捨てて秘密を守って下さるようお願いします。

Mandarin

請你騙我朋友,替我手錶調到6:42分, 以後放在手巾内,把所有鈔票拿去給你自己 謝謝.你不要告訴別人 以後把紙丟掉.

MEMO

Late-for-Lunch Miracle Maneuver

1. Sneak a fiver and your secret message onto the napkin on your lap.
2. Call over a waiter, waitress, or hostess to try a "weird psychic thing."
3. Take off your watch. Openly place it on your lap and wrap it up on your lap in the napkin (along with the secret five and the 6:42 "message"). Then bring out the bundle and hand it to the waiter.
4. Tell the waiter to go across the room, secretly set the watch to any time, wrap it back up, and bring it back to your table.
5. Set the client's watch to 6:42.
6. Tell client to unwrap your watch and watch him become unwound.
7. Secretly get a receipt from the waiter for the five bucks.

The Crispy Currency Ice Breaker

Sometimes we get so caught up in the business of business we forget that business is based on personal relationships. Unless there is a substantial price or product difference, people would rather deal with someone they like.

Before you can get a client to like you, you've got to find some common ground to advance the relationship to a more personal level—something that will bridge that gap between business and friendship.

However, sometimes just finding anything to talk about can be a monumental challenge. Now and then you've got to break all the rules to break the ice. Even if it means doing something as dramatic as defacing U.S. currency.

Problem

You're at the local power lunch palace, trying to convince yourself that eating a Caribou cutlet is a valid experience. Across the table is your potential new client slurping his cream of weasel soup. There's an awkward silence. . . . You have nothing in common, which you're kind of proud of, but still you have to break the ice and become his lunch buddy. You gently probe for some area of common interest. You try discussing sports. He hates sports. You try discussing his family. He hates his family. You try discussing his inability to communicate. He doesn't want to talk about it.

There's only one thing left that's guaranteed to break the ice. That's right. It's time to deface some U.S. currency.

Solution

Slap a dollar bill on the table and comment that there's a new version of liars' poker going around. Have your client write down the bill's serial number and tell him to drop the bill into an ashtray.

"In this new version of liars' poker if you're caught bluffing you have to burn your bill."

You take out a match, light it, and ignite the bill. Yes. I'm serious. You really torch the bill. *Poof!* Up in flames. Toast city. The client watches in disbelief as the genuine U.S. currency is cremated into a pile of smoldering ashes. No question about it. You've got the client's attention. He'll then say something like "You crazy son of a bitch." And there you have it—the client is talking to you. The ice has been broken. The conversational possibilities are endless.

But there's more. The fun has just begun.

You dump the pile of dollar ashes onto the tablecloth, splash some water onto the worthless mess, and the burnt ashes visibly transform into a complete unburned dollar bill!

You and your client now have a whole new topic of conversation to explore, and when you get tired of talking about that, have the client compare the serial number of the unburned bill with the serial number he wrote down. *The serial numbers are exactly the same! The unburned bill is the same bill you crisped a moment before.*

"Holy Moly!" Indeed yes.

Astonishing Secret

Sit down for a moment. Take a deep breath. You're about to reevaluate your attitudes about what you can and can't do with money. Are you ready? All right. Here it is. You are actually honest to god going to torch a real dollar bill and watch it go up in flames and turn into worthless ash. It's a heartstopping thrill, sort of like bungee cord jumping, except it only costs a buck and you don't have to worry if your shoes are tied.

Go to a bank where no one knows you and ask for ten *brand-new* dollar bills. The serial number of all ten new bills you receive will be *exactly the same except for the last digit*. Take the bills home, lock the door, close the shades, and put on your dark glasses.

Now take a pencil eraser and *erase* the last digit of the serial number. Yes—a normal eraser will actually erase a serial number from a dollar bill. So now instead of being 556789712 it will be 55678971. If you do this with another new bill you'll now have *two bills* with the *exact same serial number.*

Well-adjusted people have no idea how many digits are supposed to be on a bill's serial number, so when one number is missing no one will notice. With ten new bills you're able to create five sets of dollar bills with duplicate serial numbers. Put two of the duplicate bills into your wallet and you're ready to break the ice—and get a cheap thrill.

The Setup When no one's looking (or before the client arrives) sneak one of the duplicate bills under the tablecloth. Note that the bill is in front of you and opened out flat. If you're not sure you'll be able to find the exact spot where the bill is hidden, mark its location with a bread crumb or a glass of water.

When You're Ready to Break the Ice Bring the duplicate bill out of your wallet, make a few comments about liars' Poker, then have the client copy down the serial number of the bill. Tell him to drop the bill into an ashtray or a plate. Then bring out a match or lighter, wait for your hand to stop shaking, then torch the bill. If it goes out, relight it. Or if you prefer you can have the chef flambé it with some brandy.

Enjoy the adrenaline rush as the burning bill goes to fiduciary heaven, wait a moment for the ashes to cool, then dump the ashes onto the tablecloth—*right over the hidden bill.*

Splash some water over the ashes. The soaked tablecloth will instantly become *transparent*, revealing the hidden dollar and creating the startling illusion of the ashes transforming into a restored dollar!

Lift up the tablecloth, take out the moist dollar, and let your astonished client compare its serial number with the one he copied down. It's a perfect match! Everyone knows that no two bills have the same serial number. The client has no choice but to break the ice and ask how you did it.

Unfortunately you have nothing to say. You're lost in thought, wondering what it would feel like to torch a ten.

Troubleshooter

Question: What if there isn't a tablecloth?

Answer: Instead of doing the "wet tablecloth" ending you can produce the restored bill from a variety of other locations.

Before starting, fold up the duplicate bill and hide it in your shoe, tucked under your watchband, under the bread basket, inside the sugar packet caddy, or you can even arrange for the waiter to bring it over on cue. Of course you lose the visible transformation of the ashes into a whole bill, but it's still a major mini-amazer when you reveal the bill has the same serial number.

MEMO

Crispy Currency Ice Breaker

1. Get ten *brand-new* dollars from the bank (*not* an S&L).

2. Use a pencil eraser to erase the last digit from two of the dollars. Put the two bills with the same serial number into your wallet.

3. When no one is looking sneak one of the bills under the tablecloth in front of you (or some other sneaky location).

4. Bring the other bill out of your wallet and have your client copy down the serial number.

5. Put the bill on an ashtray or plate and burn the bill.

6. Sprinkle the ashes on the tablecloth over the hidden bill, rub the ashes into the cloth, then splash some water on the ashes to produce the dollar. Pull out the restored bill. Let someone check the serial number to prove it's the same bill.

7. Don't perform this for federal employees.

The Coddled Client Tabletop Fire Walk

Keeping the client happy is a highly regarded executive skill. But it's often a matter of conscience versus accommodation. Where does one draw the line?

The way out is usually a sense of humor and a realistic appeal to the client's sense of fair play.

Here's a unique lunch situation where you can keep the client coddled without getting burned.

Problem

Your lunch client is an avid seminar attendee. He is into every form of body, mind, and bladder control known to mankind. He's a self-improvement power freak. It's kind of annoying to be around him. But that's why you get paid the big bucks.

He's just completed the fire-walk seminar in the name of executive development, and only screamed in pain once. And now he wants you to do it with him, to prove that you've got the right stuff. You sense a crucial matter of client coddling is at stake. You've got to convince him that you can take the heat, yet keep your baby-smooth skin intact. What to do, what to do. . . .

Solution

You comment that barbecuing your favorite body parts is fine for amateur self-improvement buffs. But if you are really serious about becoming the very best possible you, you must spend two years at a Himalayan hermitage in a Motel 6 in order to learn the inner secrets of actually *healing* your barbecued body parts.

You demonstrate by lighting a match, then pinch out the flame with your bare fingers. You turn your finger over to reveal a *major water blister*, a first degree owie. You then close your eyes, hum a Himalayan chant, whistle the Motel 6 theme song, slowly massage the blister with your thumb, and then give your client the finger to examine. Your charbroiled flesh has undergone massive self-improvement. The skin is now smooth and pink—radiantly healthy—*the blister is gone*. You tell the client to get up off his knees—you don't like to mix business and worship.

Astonishing Secret

Don't panic! You never really burn yourself. You never have a real blister. It's all painlessly accomplished by an old Himalayan hermit trick where you create an *optical illusion blister*. The secret is actually too good to give away, but you caught me at a weak moment. (Yes, I'm going to a self-improvement seminar to work on this very problem.)

All right, here it is. To create your very own personal optical illusion blister, get hold of a key—that's right, your basic key chain key. Look at the hole in the key. If it's a *round hole* you've got a good key. If it has a square or triangle hole, put the key back and find one with a round hole. You need a key with a *round hole*.

To make the optical illusion blister, press the round hole of the key against the fleshy tip of your first finger so that you can see a tiny circle of pink stuff through the hole (Figure 3-2). Press on the key's hole against your fingertip *really hard* for about *ten seconds*. Take away the key and there you have it—*instant blister*. Don't be alarmed, it's only a toy. Now massage the blister with your thumb for about ten seconds, and in a spontaneous act of self-improvement, the blister will melt away, leaving you with a happy and glad blister-free finger.

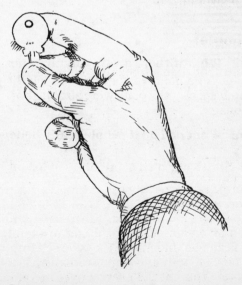

Figure 3-2

Doing It   Just before you are ready to begin, hold a key under the table (or in your pocket) and secretly create the optical illusion blister on your left first finger. Bring out your hand. Don't worry, *no one* will notice the blister until you want them to.

Light a match. Now if you're brave you can really snuff the flame with your fingers by pinching the lit match head *very fast* between your thumb and blister finger.

Warning   Your fingers should touch the lit match head for only a *fraction of an instant*. We're talking a nanosecond here. If you pinch it for too long you will hear a sizzling sound, and notice that you now have two blisters on your finger. This is one trick you don't want to learn. To be extra safe secretly lick your fingers before snuffing the flame.

Ultra-Safe Method   If snuffing a live flame with your bare fingers unsettles you, do this. Light the match, blow out the flame, and keep blowing on the burned match head "to make it really hot." What happens is that the match head actually gets really cold, so now you can safely press your finger against the "super hot burning coals." The rest is pure salesmanship. Show off your blistered finger, bravely smile through the pain, massage it with your thumb, and prepare to be worshiped.

Troubleshooter

Question: What if there aren't any matches around?
Answer: Order a hot meal for lunch, touch the plate, jerk your hand back as if the plate were sizzling hot, then show off your blister.

Question: What do I do if people really believe I healed myself?
Answer: Start your own seminar—sell lots of books and tapes.

MEMO

Client Loyalty Tabletop Fire Walk

1. Press a key with a round hole against the tip of your first finger to create a secret "optical illusion blister."
2. Light a match, snuff the flame with your fingers or blow the flame out and blow on the burned match to "make it hotter." Pretend to sizzle your finger on the burned match head.
3. Show off your blister.
4. Massage blister with your thumb for instant healing.
5. Start your own seminars.

The Client Confidence Sugar Shocker

Identifying what your customer *really* wants is usually the key to success. Maybe it's the product or service you offer, or maybe something entirely different. It might be the feeling of self-importance, respect, or just plain confidence that they are making the proper decision.

Problem

Your prospective client thinks you're swell. However, he tells you he can't write you a check containing more than one zero until he has a bit more confidence in the relationship. He needs to feel that special connection between corporate compadres before he can make a giant killer deal with you. Highly frowned upon four-, five-, and six-letter words struggle to escape from your mouth as you pray to the lunch gods for a miracle to convince the client he's lucky to know you.

Solution

To prove the lunch gods are smiling on this relationship you play a simple game of chance.

The game starts when you write a secret prediction on the back of a sugar packet and drop it in the client's pocket. In certain cultures this act alone is considered a meaningful experience.

You then grab nine other sugar packets and openly write a different number on each—from one to nine.

The numbered packets are dropped into a glass, shaken by the client like a bunch of dice, then tossed out onto the table. As fate would have it, some of the packets land with their numbered sides showing, some land with the blank side showing. You eliminate all the blank-side up packets and put the remaining number-side up packets back into the glass.

The suspense-filled shake and toss elimination game continues until one lone sugar packet remains. A single sacred sugar packet selected by the lunch gods. It happens to have the lucky number 2 written on it.

Why is this number 2 so lucky? Because the number 2 is the exact same number you wrote on the sugar packet that's still tucked in the client's pocket! An obvious omen that the lunch gods approve of the 2 of you in this relationship.

The client reaches into his other pocket and whips out a blank check. He trusts you to fill in the appropriate amount. You practice writing teeny tiny zeroes.

Astonishing Secret

One sugar packet has the lucky 2 on both sides. It is never eliminated because it doesn't have a blank side. So despite its best efforts the number 2 sugar will always be the last one on the table.

Before You Start   When no one is looking, secretly draw a 2 on one side of a sugar packet, then stuff it back in with the other sugars so the 2 doesn't show. Make sure it is the second packet in. Do this before the client arrives or while he's on the phone or in the bathroom. No one should see you fiddle with the sugar packets before your performance.

When You're Ready to Be Astonishing   Remove one of the *blank* sugar packets and draw a 2 on one side of the packet so the client can't see what you're writing. Then drop it in the client's pocket. Now pull out eight or nine other packets, including the secretly prepared 2 packet. Make sure to keep the 2 side hidden, so the client thinks all the packets are normal. Openly draw a different number on each packet from 1 to 9 and when you get to the secret 2 packet, openly draw a matching 2 on the visible side. The client will think that this 2 packet has a blank side just like the others.

Drop all of the packets including the double 2 into a big glass. Give the glass to your client. Tell him to cover the top with his hand and shake the cup up and down to mix things up, then spill all the packets onto the table. Some packets will land blank-side up (maybe one, maybe seven, you never know), and some will land number-side up. Remove all the *blank*-side up packets and toss them aside.

They're eliminated—gone—never to be seen again. Scoop all the packets with the numbers still showing back into the cup for another shake-up by the client. He spills the mixed packets back on the table and again you toss out all the blank-side up packets, leaving just the "numbers up" packets on the table. Then scoop the packets back into the cup for yet another shakeup by the client, who spills out the sugar packets again. Where you eliminate the blanks again.

That's it. Just keep playing the game—shaking, spilling, and eliminating the blanks—until only *one number-side up packet remains on the table*. That last number will *always* be the *2*. Tear open this packet (careful to keep the second *2* hidden) and dump the sugar granules into your coffee or tea. Crumple the torn packet to destroy the guilty evidence. Direct your lunch buddy to look at the secret sugar packet prediction in his pocket for the sugar shocker finale.

Troubleshooter

Question: What happens if someone picks up the double *2* packet and sees the extra *2* on the other side?

Answer: This would be a major no-no, and it won't happen as long as *you* control the sugar packets. *You* write on the packets, *you* scoop them up, and *you* eliminate the blanks.

Question: What if when the packets are dumped out *none* of the blank sides is up?

Answer: That does happen; just put them back in the cup and do it again.

Question: What happens if when the packets are dumped out, none of the number sides is up?

Answer: That is not a possibility, unless you forgot to put a second *2* on the double-*2* packet.

MEMO

Client Confidence Sugar Shocker

1. Wait for a moment until you are alone at the table (or when you're sure no one is watching you) and draw a secret 2 on one of the sugar packets. Put the marked packet back in the holder with the other sugars so the 2 doesn't show to the client. It should be the second one in. Keep an eye on the secret sugar so you can find it later.

2. Pull out one of the blank sugars and draw a 2 on one side of the packet, so that no one can see what the number is. Put this mystery prediction in the client's pocket for safekeeping.

3. Pull out eight or nine sugars, including the one with the secret 2, keep an eye on this packet so you know which one it is.

4. Openly draw a different number on one side of each of the sugars, making sure to draw a matching 2 on the blank side of the secret 2 sugar packet. Try not to look guilty.

5. Scoop all the marked sugars from the table into a glass or cup, give the cup to the client to shake and dump.

6. Discard all the blank-side up sugars.

7. Scoop the remaining sugars into the cup, repeat the shake, dump, and discard sequence until only one number-side up sugar is left. It will be a 2. Tear the 2 packet open and dump the sugar granules into your tea or coffee. Then crumple the empty packet to destroy the guilty evidence.

8. Tell the client to bring out the secret prediction from his pocket to reveal the matching lucky number 2.

9. Try to explain to the waiter why you've numbered all the sugar packets.

The Instant Client Dependency Syndrome

One mark of a successful executive is that his clients and peers think of him as a trusted ally. It's a relationship based on mutual respect, usually formed by years of working together.

But sometimes you have only minutes to establish a working rapport with someone you have just begun to work with.

One of the quickest ways to transform a total stranger into a trusted ally is to find a way to make him look good in front of others, or better yet, help him to look downright astounding.

Problem

Lunch is almost over. The client thinks you're neat—you've become official lunch buddies. But you don't want him to just like and respect and admire you—no, no, no—you want him to be dependent upon you. You want him to need your special skills so badly that he considers you a permanent part of his wardrobe. You want to create a Client Dependency Syndrome, but let's face it, he just doesn't need you that badly. No one needs you that badly. Except maybe your dog. And you're not even sure about him.

Solution

You teach your client a special trick. His employees and associates think he's the greatest. You get him hooked on the adrenaline rush of being astonishing. There's just one catch—he needs a genuine astonishing executive to do the secret part. That's right—he needs you to make him look astonishing. Voilà! Instant Client Dependency Syndrome.

Here's How It Looks   The client is at lunch and announces his famous salt shaker miracle. He covers an ordinary salt shaker with a napkin, and to be extra fair he allows everyone at the table to reach under the napkin and feel the salt shaker. There is no question of trickery—they all agree there is a salt shaker under the napkin. The client says the magic words—"Zot, whoosh, caboosh"—and the salt shaker disappears.

We're talking really gone. The crowd is genuinely dumbfounded.

The client basks in the glory . . . but he can't do it without you.

Astonishing Secret

When the skeptics in the crowd feel under the napkin to make sure that the shaker is still there, the last skeptic to feel the shaker is *you*. That's right—you are there as an important associate, and when you take your turn to feel the shaker *you secretly swipe the shaker and hide it under the table.*

The client's napkin still looks like it holds a shaker because of the way you've coached him to hold his fingers on the napkin (Figures 3–3 and 3–4). The client moves the

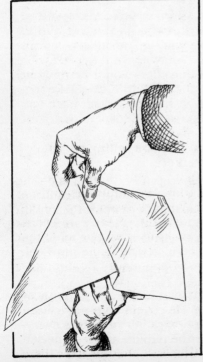

Figure 3-3

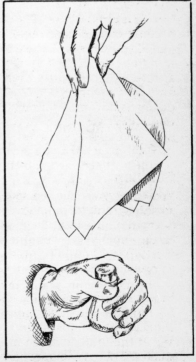

Figure 3-4

napkin-covered "salt shaker" to the center of the table, then goes for the big buildup and, whoosh, the shaker has vanished! (Figure 3-5.)

Of course, you've convinced the client it takes incredible skill to palm the shaker out of a napkin secretly, that he desperately needs you for the hard part. But only you know that you just grab the shaker and drop it on your lap.

Figure 3-5

Troubleshooter

Question: Are you serious! Are you telling me that no one will see me grab the shaker?

Answer: No one is watching you. All attention is on the holder of the napkin. You are just one of many innocent shaker feelers—and as long as the client holds the napkin at the table's edge when you steal the shaker there'll be nothing to see. You still don't believe it—Okay, stop right now. Go to lunch, find a trustworthy friend, and try it. Grab the shaker while your friend pretends it's still under the napkin and watch people's reactions. Everyone at the table will believe the salt shaker is still there. You can see it in their eyes. It's a great feeling—one your client won't forget.

Question: What do I do with the shaker in my lap?

Answer: That's between you and the shaker.

MEMO

Instant Client Dependency Syndrome

1. Offer to teach your client how to be astonishing.
2. Show him or her how to hold a napkin so it looks the same whether something is under it or not.
3. Convince the client you have special salt shaker palming skills.
4. *Do a rehearsal* where client lets you feel the napkin-covered shaker. You secretly grab it and hide it in your lap. The client pretends the shaker is still under napkin, then makes the shaker "vanish." You are now indispensable.
5. Be prepared to get invited to all of your client's important meetings.
6. Don't tell anyone how easy it is to sneak a salt shaker from under a napkin.

The Forget-Me-Not
Business Card Handout #3—
End of Lunch Sales Solidifier

Great entertainers know how to get a guaranteed standing ovation at the end of their performance. Sometimes it's a stooge in the audience who leaps to his feet at the end of the show. Sometimes it's turning up the house lights as people clap at the end to signal it's okay to get out of your seat. Whatever the method, the last image is what people remember. The entertainers arrange for a "spontaneous" reaction. They don't take a chance and neither should you.

You should always end the meeting, presentation, or business lunch with an orchestrated image of what you want your "audience" to remember.

Frequently the act of handing out your business card is the last image people have of you. You can turn this mundane moment into a memorable event by adding a touch of astonishment.

Problem

You still have a lot of business cards left after the Business Card Handout #2. Lots of little cardboard salesmen eager to praise your name and phone number to financially viable folks who would otherwise forget who you are. You continue to look for unforgettable ways to unload your business cards. Your portable pocket-size sales squad looks up to you, desperate for a chance to strut their stuff. It seems hopeless; there're so many of them. . . .

Solution

Bring out a stack of business cards carefully secured with a rubber band.

Reverently place your rubber-banded stack on the table and direct your client to press one finger onto the cards. It's now a private matter between the client and your cards. When he lifts up his finger—the stack of cards suddenly becomes alive! It spins around and squirts out one card from the side. A card personalized with the client's name. Try as he might, the client will never be able to forget you.

Astonishing Secret

Poke around in the back of your desk drawer right next to the torn stamp and the bent paper clip and find a rubber band. Snap it around a forty-card chunk of your fearless little business cards. The rubber band should be snug. If the band is too loose then double twist it around the cards.

Write "Hi, George" on one loose card, and place it *loose* on the bottom of the rubber-banded stack. The "Hi, George" card is *free and separate* from the rubber-banded stack. Hold all the cards firmly in your left hand ("Hi, George" on the bottom) as if you were going to deal a round of poker. Grab the top half of the stack with your right fingers, and stretch it to the *right*—away from the bottom of the stack (Figure 3–6). Give the top half of the stack one twist, so it's upside down as shown in Figure 3–7. Then fold it down

Figure 3-6

Figure 3-7

Figure 3-8

against the *bottom* of the other stack Figure 3–8, as you'd close a book.

You're set. Hang on tight! The cards look like a normal rubber-banded stack, but they're straining to be astonishing. Press the wound-up stack onto the table, and when you lift your finger, the rubber-banded stack will spin around and squirt out the "Hi, George" card.

Doing It for Real Pull out the banded stack (with the loose card on the bottom) and do the secret twist cut *under the table*. Bring out your "normal" stack of cards, hold them on the table, and get your client to press his finger *firmly* against the stack of cards. Quietly contemplate the perfect ending to your power lunch, then tell the client to lift his finger. Your cards will thank you.

Troubleshooter

Question: When I let go of the twisted stack it just sits there. They don't sing, they don't dance, nothing.

Answer: 1. Your rubber band is too loose or too tight. 2. You goofed up the secret twist cut. Check the illustration to make sure everything goes where it is supposed to. 3. It's just not your day.

Question: What if I'm having a gang lunch and want to give out multiple business cards in an astonishing yet businesslike manner?

Answer: Put all the cards you want to hand out *loose* on the bottom of the banded stack. Do the same secret twist cut, and multiple cards will fly out.

MEMO

The Forget-Me-Not
Business Card Handout #3—
End of Lunch Sales Solidifier

1. Snap a rubber band around forty or so business cards.
2. Put one loose "Hi, George" card under the rubber-banded stack.
3. Under-the table secret twist setup: Stretch the top half to the right (clear of the other stack), twist the top half upside down, fold it down against the bottom half, hang on tight. Bring out the twisted stack; pretend it's normal.
4. Set the stack on the table. Don't take your finger off *until* the client firmly presses a finger on top of the stack.

Bridge Burner #1—
The Bad Lunch Power Gross-Out

We all know the eighty/twenty percent rule. Eighty percent of your business comes from twenty percent of your clients. Sometimes, however, while trying to increase that twenty percent, we find we are on a bit of a wild goose chase. What hurts, though, is when your potential client leads you to believe you will be doing business together when he has known all along it will never be a "done deal." Here's something for that one percent who give you zero percent.

Problem

The client has promised you the deal of the century. You've wined and dined him for six months—the best restaurants, the best champagne, imported nachos. Finally, after months of negotiating you're ready to sign the deal. You've hocked your Hyundai to pay for this final lunch. He has a $120.00 caviar burger and you have the $70.00 fettucini with the imported shiitake mushrooms. You don't bat an eye. You give him the pen to sign the contract, and the client says, "You are a great guy—I sincerely mean that. . . . Your products are terrific. But, to be honest, I got a brother-in-law who can do the same thing for ten percent less; what can I say, family is family, but don't take it personally, I love having lunch with you." You quietly stare at him as he munches on a substantial portion of your net worth. You want to get back some of those $120.00 caviar burgers. You want revenge. . . .

Warning The following Bridge Burner was designed by the much in demand comedic corporate astonisher Mac King for use in only the most extreme bad lunch situations. It's a genuine guaranteed gross-out—and should be attempted at your own risk. If you decide to do it, please don't tell me about it.

Solution

Stare at the client . . . and start to blink. Rub your eye, fiddle with your eyelid. You're obviously in eyeball distress. Pull

Figure 3-9

your cheek down with a fork (Figure 3–9) and ask him if he sees anything in your eye. He scans your eyeball. It looks fine to him—just the white stuff. You say, "I think I can get it with the fork."

You cover your eye with one hand as your other hand holds the fork. You move the fork toward your hand-covered eye, poke in the fork, there's a "pop" sound, and a gush of white fluid squirts out and dribbles down your face. You stare at the client with your one good eye and say, "Don't you hate when that happens?" The client nods, rushes to the bathroom where he's dramatically reminded that there is no such thing as a free lunch.

The Ingeniously Gross Secret

Sneak a *sealed coffee creamer* off the table and hide it in your hand under the tabletop (Figure 3–10). Pretend there's something stuck in your eye. Really go for it, using all your latent acting skills.

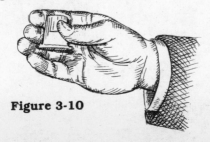

Figure 3-10

Make the client really believe you have a serious eye problem. When you're ready for the power gross-out, bring your hand out from under the table with the hidden coffee creamer, and cup your hand over the closed eye (Figure 3–11). The creamer remains hidden under your hand. With your other hand, turn your fork so the pointy ends are away from your eye. Remember to *keep your eye closed*, and with your free hand, *carefully* poke the fork under your hand to puncture the creamer seal (Figure 3–12), and, yuck, a gush of white stuff dribbles from your eye. Then expose the empty creamer and reveal it was all in good wholesome fun, if you want.

Figure 3-11

Figure 3-12

GASP FACTOR

Effectiveness Through Simplicity

The illusions you've learned create incredible impact with surprisingly simple methods.

Always look for the simplest and most direct route to accomplish your objectives and goals.

4

The Astonishing Client's Office

Make-the-Secretary-Think-You're-Swell Quasi Legal Pad Prediction

---

The client's secretary is one of the most overlooked steps to success. The secretary is usually a good barometer of what type of person your client is and how they like to conduct business. You can usually tell how the boss is going to react to you by how the secretary reacts to you. Here's an unusual gambit to increase your odds.

Problem

The secretary has the power to create or destroy. A few whispered words to the boss and you can be advanced into the "A" Rolodex or shoved back into the "What's His Name" sludge pile. Knowing this, you attempt to get on her good side, just like a thousand other sludge pile execs try to do. But you don't have anything clever to say, and you can't afford a truly meaningful bribe so you sit in the waiting room and wait and wait . . . just another sludged-out exec.

Solution

You innocently borrow a pen from the secretary. You scrutinize her face for a moment, then write "red, green, blue" on the top sheet of your legal pad. You ask if she'd like to take the personality color test. How can she refuse? You give her a wadded paper ball and tell her to drop it on "red," "green," or "blue," whichever feels psychologically correct. She drops it on "green." You tell her if another color feels more psychologically correct she should move the ball. She moves it to "blue."

You give her the option to change her mind again. She says, "No thank you; I'm happy with the mind I have." She wants "blue." She opens up the paper ball—and on it is written "Special people always choose blue." She looks at you with new interest and says, "How'd you know I'd choose blue?" You reply, "Special people always choose blue." She can't help but smile, and when no one's looking she'll sneak your Rolodex card into the "A" file.

Astonishing Secret

You have *three different secret predictions*, so no matter which of the three colors she selects you simply reveal the prediction and pretend it's the only one.

Before You Start While sitting in the waiting room, doodling on your legal pad, peel open the top page and across the back of this top page write in big print "Special people always choose red." Now, on the *same side* of the paper write on one of its *corners* "Special people always choose blue." On the other side of this corner (the "front side of the page") put a tiny dot. This way you'll always remember which corner the message is under.

So now you've got *two* secret messages on the back of the top page: One big one across the middle and one small message on a corner. (You should *not* be able to see the secret messages through the top of the sheet). Flip the entire pad over to the cardboard backing and write directly on to the cardboard "Special people always choose green."

You're all set with three secret predictions—the only evidence is a tiny ink dot in one corner on the top page.

Wander over to the official Sovereign Secretary Island and tell her you've made a secret prediction about her psychologically correct color profile. You're never wrong. Savvy super-secretary that she is, she'll demand proof. Put your quasi legal pad on her desk (keeping the secret message hidden on the backside) and carefully tear off the secret dotted corner (with the secret message hidden on the back). Wad this corner up into a little ball, careful not to reveal its secret message, and hand it to the secretary. Tell her it's the secret color selector.

Then write the three official colors on the top sheet—red, green, blue. Carefully tear off the top sheet, keeping the big secret message on the back a secret. Tell the secretary to drop her color tester wad on any color. She can move it around and change her mind as often as she wants, but must eventually stop on the one color that feels psychologically correct. You are now going to expose one of the three secret predictions, *while pretending it's the one-and-only secret prediction.*

If the secretary chooses "blue": Tell her to open the crumpled ball and read your secret prediction "Special people always choose blue."

If the secretary chooses "red": Drop the crumbled wad in the trash and tell her to turn over the paper to read your secret prediction "Special people always choose red."

If the secretary chooses "green": Crumple the three-color top sheet into a ball and toss it and the wadded corner into the trash. The only thing left is the legal pad. Tell her to turn the pad over and to read your secret prediction "Special people always choose green."

Troubleshooter

Question: What if the secretary wants to see it again?

Answer: Tell her it wouldn't be psychologically valid a second time—since you both already know what her correct color is.

Question: Can I do it with more than three colors?

Answer: Sure—you just need more secret predictions. You can have a fourth prediction rolled up inside the pen cap, a fifth prediction on the back of a $20 bill (which, you tell her, you'll give her if you predict *wrong*).

MEMO

Quasi Legal Pad Predictions

1. While doodling on your legal pad write three secret predictions: across the *back of the top sheet*, "Special people always choose red"; on the back of the *top sheet corner* write "Special people always choose blue" (put a dot on top to mark the corner); on the cardboard back-side of the pad write "Special people always choose green."

2. Approach the secretary, tear off the dotted corner, careful to keep its hidden message concealed, crumble it into a ball, and give it to the secretary to hold.

3. Openly write "red," "green," "blue" on the top sheet. Rip it out (be careful not to reveal the secret prediction on the back) and place it on the desk.

4. Tell the secretary to drop her ball on any color, and move the ball to different colors until "she feels psychologically correct."

5. If she chose "blue": open ball, trash the sheet; if she chose " red": turn over paper, trash the ball; if she chose " green": trash the ball and the sheet and turn over the pad.

6. Don't forget secretary's week.

The Hard-to-Ignore Off-the-Wall Office Entrance

The businessman who enters someone else's office with his shirt hanging out, slumped shoulders, and sweaty palms, begging for a moment of their time, usually gets that—a moment of their time.

When you enter someone's life, think about the image you're creating. That image could last a lifetime.

Problem

You enter the client's office. She eagerly glances up then goes back to her work. False alarm—she confused you with the guy who delivers her wrestling magazines. The client says you'll have to wait until she completes an urgent $1 million deal. You can't help but notice the "Publishers Clearing House Sweepstakes" on her desk. You sigh, sit down on a little stool in the corner, make a few hand shadows to amuse yourself, and wonder where you went wrong.

Solution

You simply need to make a more dynamic, thought-provoking, awe-inspiring entrance something like this: The client is sitting in her office, focused on her "Publishers Clearing House Sweepstakes," when she hears a weird thump on the wall. She looks up, and sees a human hand grasping the top edge of the doorjamb (Figure 4–1). A second hand appears and grasps the top edge of the doorjamb (Figure 4–2). It seems that someone outside the office is stuck to the top of the wall—her curiosity is piqued. And then from between the two hands, a head pokes out from the top of the doorjamb (Figure 4–3). No doubt about it there *is* someone stuck to the top of the wall outside her office door. It's you. You suddenly let go—and disappear from view as if something pulled you across the wall. The bewildered client has a burning desire to know just what the heck happened, when you casually walk in standing on your own two feet. She gives you her desk and sits down on the little stool in the corner prepared to listen to anything you might have to say.

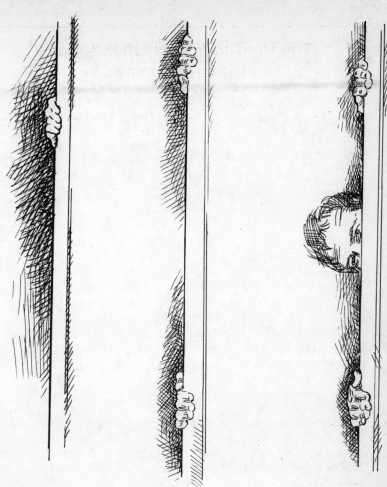

Figure 4-1   **Figure 4-2**   **Figure 4-3**

Astonishing Secret

It's easy, all you have to do is bend your body and stand on one foot as shown in Figure 4–4 to create the illusion that you're a wacky wall walker. Don't worry, I'll walk you through it step by step.

To start, knock on the wall near the door to get her attention. Then, press against the wall next to the open door. Then reach out with one hand and clutch the doorjamb as high up as you can get (Figure 4–5). Make it a dramatic grab—as if you're doing a strenuous one-hand pull-up. Then stand on one foot—and stretch the other leg out along the wall. A second later clutch the doorjamb with your other hand (Figure 4–6). The people inside will see two hands clutching the doorway. Yes, you'll have their attention. Then with "incredible effort" do your sideways "pull-up" so your head pokes out between your two hands. Hold the pose for a second or two, stare at the gaping people in the room, then release your grip on the doorjamb and "stay bent" as you pull yourself away from the doorjamb out of sight, and apparently "fall across the wall." Once you're out of sight regain your two-footed balance. Then walk into the office as if nothing happened.

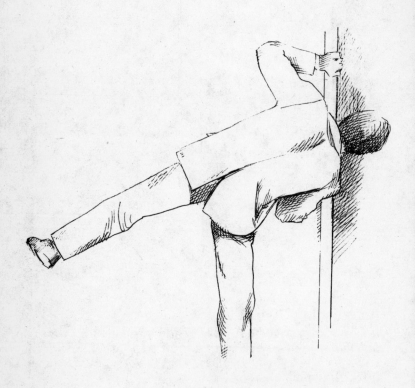

Figure 4-4

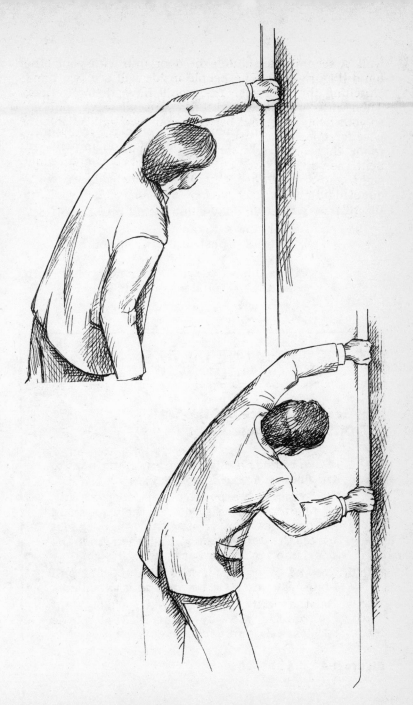

Figure 4-6

Troubleshooter

Question: What do you mean "fall across the wall"?
Answer: I was afraid you'd ask that. You can't really fall across the wall, but then again, you can't really crawl across the wall either. For the sake of astonishment, you are creating the illusion that the wall is part of a unique gravity system where when you fall you don't fall down, you fall across.

Question: What do I say when I walk into the office?
Answer: 1. "Hi, how's it going?"
2. "I think I pushed the wrong button on the elevator."
3. Nervously close the door, catch your breath, and say, "You don't want to know."

MEMO

Hard-to-Ignore Off-the-Wall Office Entrance

1. When outside a client's office, stand next to the door so no one inside can see you.

2. Dramatically grasp high on the doorjamb with one hand. Then press against the wall, stand on one foot, and stretch the other leg out across the wall. Wait a second, then grasp the doorjamb with the other hand.

3. Pretend to do a sideways pull-up, and pull your head into view, between your two hands.

4. Release your hands and fall out of sight "across the wall" by sliding back along the wall then regaining your balance.

5. Stand up straight, walk into the office as if nothing happened.

6. Don't throw away your "Publishers Clearing House Sweepstakes" . . . you never know.

The One-Too-Many-Interruptions Ravaged Office Revenge

When you're being ignored or interrupted, sometimes you have to take extreme measures to command the attention you deserve.

Problem

The client interrupts your presentation for the eighteenth time by taking yet another phone call. You smile, shrug it off—"No problem." When the client's back is turned you make icky faces, crude gestures, and silently mouth the word chowderhead. Boy, if only there were a more effective way to vent your frustrations and get his attention.

Solution

When your less-than-attentive client turns to answer the phone for the nineteenth time, secretly peel away a three-inch area of paint or wallpaper from his wall. Play innocent while the client has a screaming hissy fit over the irreparable damage.

After you've extracted your revenge, calmly press your hand against the tear and miraculously and instantly heal the defaced wall to its original unripped glory. The phone rings—the client rips it out of the wall. He'd rather talk to you.

Astonishing Secret

The heart-stopping rip is not a rip at all. There is no damage to the wall whatsoever. The thing that looks exactly like ripped wallpaper or peeled paint is actually an optical illusion rip—created by a torn piece of Post-it. "Really? A Post-it?" That's right, an ordinary Post-it impersonates an unsightly rip. Yes, it boggles the mind. But you should be getting used to this by now.

Before You Start You'll need a white or light brown Post-it. Peel off a Post-it, and fold it in half as in Figure 4–7. The sticky stuff is on the *outside*.

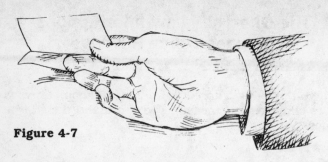

Figure 4-7

Tear the sticky section off the Post-it (Figure 4–8). Then from this one torn sticky strip, tear off a thin slice from both sides, so that the edges are jagged (Figure 4–9). Finally, curl one of the wings down as shown in Figure 4–10. Donate the rest of the Post-it to a less astonishing exec.

You should now have a jagged-edged sticky piece of Post-it, with the sticky stuff on the outside.

Doing It Look around to make sure no one is looking, then stick the straight, uncurled, sticky side to the wall. Congratulations—you've created an instant optical illusion rip. Wait for your client to notice the rip—let the panic build to a crescendo—then reveal your knack for solving problems.

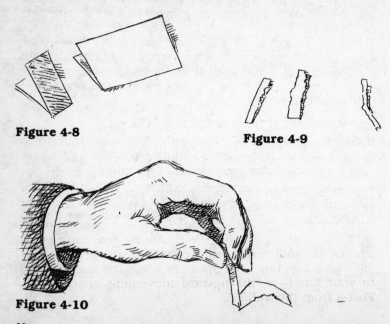

Figure 4-8

Figure 4-9

Figure 4-10

Figure 4-11

Smush your palm flat against the curl so the sticky stuff sticks to your palm (Figure 4–11), then slide your palm *up* against the wall. Keep sliding your hand up until the rip unsticks from the wall and secretly sticks to your palm.

Slowly pull your hand away (keeping the palmed Post-it hidden) to reveal the results of your astonishing problem-solving skills. While everyone's examining your incredible fix-it job you'll have plenty of time to secretly peel off the palmed Post-it and stick it in your pocket.

Troubleshooter

Question: What if no one notices the rip?

Answer: Comment to your client, "You know that really doesn't look too bad—you can hardly notice it." He'll say, "Notice what?" and you're off and running.

Question: When I move my hand away from the rip, it's still stuck to the wall. Why is this?

Answer: First, make sure your palm is in direct contact with the sticky side of the curl, then press your palm against the wall *very hard*. Keep the pressure on as you slide your hand up—the pressure keeps the Post-it stuck to your hand—as the upward movement unsticks the Post-it from the wall.

Question: What if I forget to bring my Post-its?

Answer: An astonishing executive *never* forgets his Post-its, but if the unthinkable happens, it is possible to rig up a non-Post-it version.

Create the optical illusion rip from a white *unprinted* section of newspaper. Curl one "wing" just as you did with the Post-it, then moisten the back of the flat "wing" with your tongue and stick it to the wall. (The paper, not your tongue.) If it doesn't stick, you will have to apply additional moisture. This can get pretty disgusting, but that's the price you pay for forgetting your Post-its.

To "heal" the rip, give your palm a good wet lick and press your moistened palm flat against the rip (don't worry about the curl), slide your hand up the wall, and you're back in business.

MEMO

The One-Too-Many-Interruptions Ravaged Office Revenge

1. Fold a Post-it in half and rip out a set of "sticky wings" so the sticky stuff is on the outside.
2. Curl up one "wing" so it looks like the peeled part of a rip.
3. Make sure no one is watching, then stick the *flat* "wing" against the wall.
4. Heal the rip by pressing your palm against the sticky side of the curl, pressing everything against the wall.
5. Press very hard as you slide your palm *up* the wall, to secretly stick the Post-it to your palm while unsticking it from the wall.
6. Move your hand away from the wall (keeping the palm-stuck Post-it hidden).
7. When everyone's looking at the healed wallpaper, secretly pocket the palmed Post-it.
8. Don't ever forget your Post-its.

The Buck Stops Here $100 Visualizer

Dramatize your ideas. You are one step closer to a sale if you can visually demonstrate what the end result of the product or service will do for the client. And if you help the client visualize the financial benefits, he just might close the deal for you.

Problem

The basic problem of all problems—convincing a client that you are the one exec in a thousand who actually knows how to make money. You show him beautiful brochures, with nifty financial graphs and video presentations with animated dollar signs that do the tango. The client just sits there and yawns.

Solution

You take out a single dollar bill, say the magic word "R.O.I." and proceed to turn the buck into a piece of the American dream—a genuine $100 bill. The client chortles with delight, slaps you on the back, causing you to spit out your Tums. The client begs you to turn *his* dollar into a $100. You shake him off your foot and say, "Hey, why bother with small change? Let's sign the deal and make you some real money." The client rereads your four-color brochure with new enthusiasm. You quietly retrieve your Tums and try to remember what R.O.I. means.

Astonishing Secret

Basically it's a sneaky way of switching in a $100 bill. I know you were hoping you could just sort of poof the $100 bill from the ozone—unfortunately you've got to acquire the $100 bill first.

Before You Start   You have to rubber cement a $1 bill to a $100 bill. Rubber cement unsticks and rubs off, so don't worry, your Ben Franklin will be just fine. The rubber cement, however, is permanently ruined.

If the idea of dabbing rubber cement on a $100 bill makes you feel icky, you can use a $50, $20, $10 or one of those green coupons offering twenty percent off on a lube job.

Making the $100 Change-O Bill In this description I'll pretend you're using a $100 bill because it makes me feel special.

Step 1. Holding the $1 bill in your hands so that the George Washington side faces the floor, fold the $1 bill in half from end to end, and in half again in the same direction, and in half a third time from the top down in quarters (Figures 4–12, 4–13 and 4–14). Fold the $100 bill exactly the same way. From now on, whenever you fold or unfold these bills, they will always be in this fashion, along these precreased lines.

Step 2. Unfold the $1 bill so it is facedown and smear a thin coat of rubber cement on the lower right "square" (Figure 4–15). Place the folded $100 bill onto the rubber cement square as in Figure 4–16 so the loose floppy ends of the $100 bill are pointing up and away from the center of the $1 bill.

Line up the folded $100 bill with the square corner of the $1 bill for as perfect a match as possible. If you've messed

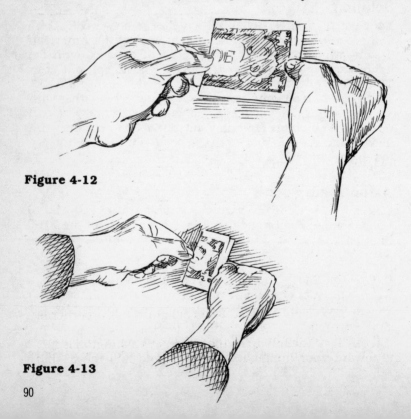

Figure 4-12

Figure 4-13

Figure 4-14

Figure 4-15

Figure 4-16

up, don't panic. Just peel of the $100 bill, rub off the rubber cement, and try again.

Great. You've got a folded $100 bill glued to the corner of a folded $1 bill.

Step 3. Pick the bill up so that George Washington is facing toward your imaginary audience and fold the $1 bill along the creases (over to the right, again to the right, and then down) so that you are holding two squares of money. Stick the folded double bill under a heavy object like a portable computer or your stack of "Macaroni Buyers Monthly." Take a walk, have a root beer, come back and retrieve your flattened double bill.

Your change-o bill should be ready for action. If extra rubber cement squished out of the edges, just rub it off with your fingers.

Step 4. Unfold the $1 bill (the $100 bill stays folded). Sit in a nice comfy chair and prepare for a rehearsal session. This is the one thing in the book that actually requires a little chunk of time to learn. It's an easy sequence—just folding and unfolding the bills—but it has to be done in a certain way, and your fingers will have to fold and unfold the bills about fifteen times so this certain way becomes automatic. After a short rehearsal, you will have mastered the profitable art of turning a $1 bill into a $100 bill.

The $100 Bill Rehearsal Session

Step 1. Fold the $1 bill twice so it looks like Figure 4–17. The quartered $100 bill is hidden at the back and held between both hands. This is the official starting position. You'll always start this way and end this way. Look at your double bills. Look at your fingers. These are your friends. Be happy.

Step 2. Unfold the $1 bill with your left fingers. Your right fingers hang onto the secret corner, your right thumb keeps the folded $100 bill from flapping around. No biggy—you've unfolded a $1 bill so people think it's just a $1 bill.

Step 3. You are about to show the other side of the $1 bill so the folks at home know everything is Okay. The back right square of the $1 bill with the glued, folded $100 bill is secretly transferred to the left fingers as in Figure 4–18. You are simply turning the $1 bill around to show its other side, making sure the folded $100 bill remains hidden under your fingers as in Figure 4–19.

Step 4. Reverse the movements to turn the face of the $1 bill back to the front.

Step 5. Your left fingers fold the bill in half—left to right. Then fold it in half again to the "official position." Fold the $1 bill down so the folded $1 bill and the secret $100 bill are the same size. Then turn the whole thing over, so the $100 bill is at the front and the $1 bill is at the back. Everything still looks fine from the front—just a square of folded green money.

Figure 4-17

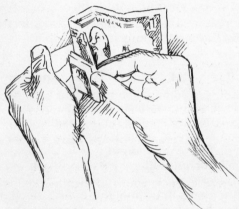

Figure 4-18

Figure 4-19

Step 6. Allow the folded $100 bill to "pop open" at the bottom so your left fingers can easily unfold it while your right fingers hang onto the secretly folded $1 bill on the back. Show both sides of the $100 bill—just as you did before with the $1 bill, but this time keeping the folded one dollar bill hidden.

Yes, you've done it! You've shown both sides of a $1 bill, folded it up, and unfolded it into a $100 bill. Put your newfound wealth back into your pocket.

Step 7. Run through all six steps in a mirror until you can change a $1 bill into a $100 bill and astonish yourself.

Troubleshooter

Question: Do you really expect me to memorize all these little details so everything comes out right?

Answer: No. You don't have to memorize anything— simply by following the instructions and rehearsing the sequence, your *fingers* will memorize the details for you.

Question: What if someone wants to examine the $100 bill?

Answer: People are usually too surprised to think about that. Remember, you've already shown both sides of the $100 bill—it all seems very fair—and as soon as you've shown both sides you fold it up and put it in your pocket. *Now* if someone insists on handling the $100 you say "No problem" and pull a *normal* $100 bill out of the same pocket (which just happens to be folded the same way as the special bill still safe and sound in your pocket).

MEMO

The Buck Stops Here $100 Visualizer

1. Rubber cement a folded $100 bill to the back of a $1 bill as described under Astonishing Secret.

2. Practice steps 1 through 7 until your fingers and the bills have become close friends.

3. Try to remember what R.O.I. means.

The I-Forgot-to-Do-My-Homework
Annual Report Cover-up

A pitcher never starts a game without knowing the other team's lineup. Who swings at high fast balls and who goes for low breaking balls. Before you walk in, know everything you can about their company, the key players, what drives them, what their past is like, how they see the future, and who are the decision makers. If you want to win, you have to do your homework.

Problem

You're in the client's office to present the giant killer proposal of all proposals. You've had six months to prepare. Six months to learn about your client's special needs. Six months to immerse yourself in the heart, soul, and pancreas of his company. And today's the big day to regurgitate all this useless information.

There's just one little snag—you forgot to do your homework. For the last six months you've been studiously assembling a Tyco Speedmaster slot car track around your office. And you haven't the foggiest notion about what the client's company is about. And now if you don't convince him that you've done your homework you'll lose the bid and quite possibly have to pawn your Speedmaster.

Solution

Enter your client's office and reverently bring out the last three issues of the company's annual report. Already he's impressed. No one's ever bothered to read them before. You must be a special breed indeed. You explain that not only have you read the company's annual reports—you've committed every word to memory.

To prove your superior homework skills, the client picks up any one of the three different annual reports, opens it to any page, and secretly counts down to a word. Without any excuses you instantly recite the word he's looking at. The client is astonished. He still can't believe that anyone would actually read their annual reports. And then he recognizes the Tyco X28 Executive Speedmaster slot car in your pocket. He whips out his Remco H71 slot car Superchief.

He trashes the annual reports as the two of you compare wheelies.

Astonishing Secret

All three annual reports are the same; they just look different.

Before You Start Obtain *three duplicate annual reports* from last year and *two* different annual reports from the two previous years.

Remove the covers from *two* of the *duplicates* (pry out the staples first) throw the covers away so you don't get confused.

Next, remove the covers from the two different reports and *keep the covers*; throw away the relatively worthless report part.

Quick inventory:

- Three exact duplicate annual reports. Only one of them still has a cover;
- Two different report covers that don't match anything;
- A trashcan full of reports, covers, and bent staples.

Restaple the two different report covers over the two uncovered duplicates. Hot dog—you now have *three duplicate* current annual reports that look exactly like *three different* annual reports from the outside. Homework's over.

When You Are Ready to Be Astonishing Bring out the three "different" annual reports, drop them on the client's desk, and tell him to pick up any one he wants. Don't worry about him leafing through and discovering it's not the right one: (1) Very few execs know what the company's annual report is supposed to look like; (2) The one or two execs who were bored enough to read the report have not committed every page to memory; (3) Each annual report includes figures from previous years, so all annual reports in any year look remarkably similar to any other year; (4) Relax. If I said no one will notice—it must be true.

All right, the client holds what he firmly believes is one of three different annual reports. Ask him to name any number, let's say twelve, and to open the report to page twelve, so that you can't see the page.

You casually demonstrate with one of the *other* reports

by opening it so he can't see what page you're on. The client thinks you are innocently opening the report to illustrate your point. But you're not that innocent—you boldly open it to his same page twelve, giving you *instant access* to the same information your client has. Tell him to count to the twelfth word on the page—*demonstrate by counting out loud to your twelfth word* (don't say the word). Tell your client to remember his twelfth word (which you cleverly remember also). Casually toss your report aside and tell the client to close his report. You then tell him the exact word he was looking at—proving that no one does their homework better than an astonishing exec.

Troubleshooter

Question: What if I can't get a hold of their annual reports?

Answer: It will still work with the company's 10Qs or 10ks.

Question: What if the client is so impressed he wants me to do it again?

Answer: You might get away with this a second time, and then again you might not. If you don't feel lucky put the three annual reports back in your briefcase and say that you're here to solve his problems—not show off. Apologize for your moment of immodesty, and if he still demands more astonishment, show him one of your other mini-amazers.

Question: Is there a way I can do it without using annual reports?

Answer: Just rig three different magazines the same way and you can stun passersby with your in-depth knowledge of current affairs.

MEMO

The I-Forgot-My-Homework
Annual Report Cover-up

1. Staple three different report covers onto three duplicate annual reports (one will be unchanged).

2. Let the client select one annual report, then pick one up yourself to "demonstrate" the procedure. "Name any page number (such as twelve), turn to that page so I can't see it, count down to the twelfth word, remember it, and close your cover."

3. As you demonstrate the above directions with your "different" report, secretly turn to page twelve and note the twelfth word.

4. Put the three reports back into your briefcase, smile knowingly, then tell the client the twelfth word on page twelve, to prove you've done your homework.

The Burbling of a Pea

Pay attention to the client's kids. Get them on your side. If the children like you and look forward to seeing you, your dealings with their parents will be a lot easier.

Problem

You're at your client's house for dinner and his nine-year-old refuses to eat his peas. The client has to exercise his parental power and insist the kid eat his peas. The kid has to be true to his tastebuds and spits a pea in Dad's face. Dad says, "Eat your peas or no MTV." The kid threatens Dad with a fistful of mashed potatoes. You sense your relaxed deal-making ambiance is about to be compromised.

Solution

You bring the hostilities to an abrupt halt by performing a curious levitation of a small vegetable. Wherein you float a pea half an inch in the air above your lips. A curious sight indeed. The father-son conflict is forgotten. Dad turns the TV back on. Junior puts down his congealed weapon. And all three of you "burble a pea." Laughter and joy abound. Peas fly all over the place. The deal-making ambiance is back. You're way ahead of the game and they haven't even seen what you can do with Jell-O cubes.

Astonishing Secret

Well, it's not all *that* astonishing but it is fun—a lot more fun than eating your peas.

Burbling a pea is the human equivalent of floating a Ping-Pong ball on a jet of air above a vacuum cleaner nozzle. Years of R&D by top jet propulsion labs combined forces with the pea grower specialists to bring this space age feat to the dinner table.

Pick out the roundest smoothest pea you can find. Try to avoid a side trip into the mashed potatoes. Then tilt your head straight back—so you're looking up at the ceiling—and perch the pea on your pursed lips. Keep your head still and *don't laugh*. If you laugh the pea will fly off, or worse, it'll fall into your mouth and you'll have to eat it.

Take a deep breath through your nose, and ever so gently blow a thin stream of air up through your lips. Experiment with lip positions and air speed until the pea floats above your lips and stays suspended in thin air. At this point you can have an assistant pass a small hoop around the floating pea to prove there are no threads or wires attached. When you're out of breath let the pea gently waft down to your lips, pluck it off, and give the pea to the dog. Teach everyone else at the table to burble a pea; see if you can all get three peas burbled at once.

Troubleshooter

Question: Can the pea-burbling technique be used for other edible entries, such as Brussels sprouts or tofu melon balls?

Answer: To the best of my knowledge, burbling will only work with a pea or pealike object. Attempting to burble anything larger could be humiliating if not downright dangerous.

MEMO

The Burbling of a Pea

1. Pick out a round smooth pea.
2. Tilt your head back so you can see the ceiling.
3. Perch pea on pursed lips.
4. Gently blow a continuous stream of air to ''burble'' the pea above your lips.
5. Don't laugh.
6. Pass a hoop around the pea to prove no threads of wires are attached.

The Dance-for-Your-Dinner
Long-Distance Name Dropper

More often than not, serious business gets accomplished in not so serious business surroundings. There are no interruptions on the golf course. Diversion disappears at the theater. Sometimes it's even easier to be memorable in places where you're not expected to be memorable.

Problem

You've used strategic astonishment to get remembered and talked about by a client. And now you're at his house to sign a huge contract. A deal that will earn you a wad of money as big as your face. Your only regret is that you don't have a bigger face.

Mr. Wonderful brings out the contract, which guarantees to throw you all his new business unless he feels cranky one day and changes his mind. You're anxious to close the deal. You hold your breath as his pen hovers over the somewhat binding document, when he stops and says, "Hey . . . you know what? . . . Just for fun, I want you to do one of those astonishing mini-amazer things you're so good at. If I'm really impressed, I'll sign the deal. And if I'm not so amazed, well, we can still be pals and I'll buy you a sandwich or a yogurt or something."

Yes, it's finally happened. A direct challenge for you to be astonishing—with all the cookies at stake. You try to joke your way out of the situation. "How about if I turn your car into a driveway?" Mr. Wonderful is not amused. "Wanna see me make a dog float? You get some root beer and two scoops of dog." No dice. He wants the real thing. Hard-core astonishment—right here, right now—or he won't sign the deal. You sulk for a moment and think, I don't have to take this abuse. . . . And then you think again, "Yes, I do. . . ."

Solution

Instruct Mr. Wonderful to go into a room where there's a phone. (One of his henchmen guards you to make sure you don't listen in or pick up an extension.)

Inside the closed room he secretly phones *anyone he knows in the entire world*—in this case a guy named Sid—

and asks him to name *any* number from one to fifty. He explains the strange request by saying "It's a weird psychic experiment."

After Mr. Wonderful hears the secret number, he hangs up, walks out of the room, looks at you, and says, "So now what?"

So now you're going to try to guess what the secret number is—a secret number that is locked away in Mr. Wonderful's economy-size brain. He has to admit . . . if you could guess that number, he'd be drop-dead astonished.

You grab your trusty mind-reading paraphernalia—a glass of water, a salad fork, and an aspirin. With these simple psychic aids you go into the phone room, close the door, and do some secret psychic stuff. Strange tapping sounds are heard. A few moments later you return from the phone room. The fork is in the empty glass. The aspirin is gone. You stare at the skeptical client, and tell him that the secret number locked in his brain is the number fourteen. The awestruck client-to-be quietly gasps. Executives aren't supposed to be able to do things like that—not even astonishing ones.

You then peer at the fork in the glass, hold it near your ear, then ask the client: "Do you know anyone named Sid?"

The deranged client shrieks, "Now how did you know *that*!" You refuse to tell until he signs the deal. He hurriedly signs, and you still don't tell him . . . because now you don't have to.

Astonishing Secret

Go into the closed phone room with the aspirin, salad fork, and glass of water. Take the aspirin for your headache, drink the water, then clank the fork against the glass, to make eavesdroppers think something supernatural is going on. Your special psychic props are *red herrings*. Meaningless *camouflage* to distract the client from your *real secret*, which is based on pushing one little button.

The Real Secret Inside the closed room you pick up the phone and press the *redial button!* This built-in psychic device will instantly connect you with the secret friend dialed by your client. Talk to whoever answers the phone and explain that you're a friend of the client's. You're at his house doing this weird psychic experiment. *If* whoever answers the phone is not the person your client just talked to, that person will let you know and will then put the right person on the line.

So now, thanks to the psychic redial button, you're talking with the only other person in the world who knows what the secret number is. As you talk to this person get his or her name, and explain that you're the one who set up the "weird psychic experiment." And that you are *playing a joke* on the client.

Explain the whole thing—how the redial works, everything. Once you've got him on your side, ask him for the secret number, thank him profusely, and ask him to keep the secret so he can amaze the client the same way on his own. The friendly conspiracy is sealed. Hang up. Wipe off any fingerprints, clink the fork a few more times, then walk out of the room, fork in glass, with a psychiclike expression on your face.

You now know the unknowable. The client's secret number *and* the name of the secret person he called.

Try to be kind as you turn his brain into Liquid Paper.

Troubleshooter

Question: What if the phone doesn't have a redial button?

Answer: Don't attempt this experiment unless you feel exceptionally lucky.

Question: What if the person on the phone forgets the secret number?

Answer: Through your secret chat you should be able to get enough information to convince the client of your super phone powers. Admit to the client you couldn't pick up the secret number, then as he chuckles at your feeble excuse casually drop your other secret knowledge.

Question: What if the friend he called won't tell me?

Answer: Think about it, if you had the opportunity to pull a stunt on your best friend, would you?

Question: What if I get a busy signal, or worse, an answering machine—or even worse no one answers and the phone just rings and rings and rings?

Answer: Calm down. First, those are all *remote* possibilities. Odds are you'll connect with the person whom your client just talked to. If the phone's busy, hit redial and try again. If it's still busy, leave the room to assemble more "psychic props," kill some time, then go back to the room and try again. If the phone is still busy, or you get an answering machine or no one answers, go back to George and tell him the psychic vibrations weren't strong enough and to try the experiment with a *different* secret friend.

MEMO

Dance-for-Your-Dinner
Long-Distance Name Dropper

1. Check to make sure your client's phone has a redial button.
2. Tell the client to call anyone he wants in the world, to tell the person he's doing a weird psychic experiment, and to ask the person to name any number from one to fifty. The client is to *remember the number*, then hang up the phone and come out of the room, *without* telling you the secret number.
3. You grab some "psychic props" (use any weird combination of small household appliances that appeal to you) and go into the phone room and close the door.
4. Pick up the phone and hit the redial button. Get hold of the person who was just talking to your client, get his name, and explain that you're at the client's house "doing the weird psychic experiment"—and it's all to play a joke on the client. Explain the whole scam, then get him to divulge the secret number.
5. Ask the person to keep your secret, thank him, hang up, then leave the room and read your client's mind.

Bridge Burner #2—
Memory-O-Matic

Forgetting the names of important clients can be one of the most embarrassing and uncomfortable situations in business. Here's a unique solution to a nameless problem.

Problem

You have read all of the mnemonic methods for remembering names. Frank—envision him dripping with sauerkraut and mustard. Carol—picture her as a singing Christmas tree. Chuck —chopped steak. Bill—a giant dollar. By the end of the day you can't remember why you put mustard on a Christmas tree and why you put Carol in a vat of sauerkraut.

Solution

Our secret technique on the other hand, takes zero effort, and while not surefire, it is certainly memorable.

Step 1: You are at a cocktail party and someone says to you, "Hi. My name's George."

Step 2: You instantly reply, "Well, hey, that's my name too!" Whoever you meet, whatever they say their name is, always reply, "Well, hey, that's my name too!"

Step 3: An hour later, one of the thousands of people you've met comes up to you and says, "Hi, George."

Step 4: The Memory-O-Matic system kicks in, your brain cells are energized, and with total recall you reply, "Hi, George."

Literally millions of important names can be memorized this way—making that one-in-a-million client feel extra special.

Editors Note Use the Memory-O-Matic system at your own risk. Awkward situations may arise when being introduced to the opposite sex, large groups of people, or when two strangers are attempting to use the Memory-O-Matic system on each other.

GASP FACTOR

A Window of Opportunity

At the moment of astonishment a client's defenses are down. His mind is totally accessible to positive information.

That window of astonishment remains open for several moments. Any information you mention at that time will be absorbed and remembered by the client's subconscious.

5

The Astonishing Negotiator

The Good Faith Negotiation Neutralizer

Never, but never, negotiate on a full stomach. After eating, you're not as sharp or alert as when you are hungry. But when it's time to negotiate what to eat, you should let your stomach do the talking.

Problem

Eight negotiators are sitting around a conference table that's much too big for any practical purpose. The last important round of negotiations begin. What to order for lunch—Chinese or Mexican, deli or pizza, sushi or Swedish, Cantonese or macrobiotic? Normally you would carefully consider everyone's opinions. Study the options. Compromise on your compromise. Give and take. Go for the win-win scenario. But you don't want to debate it. You want Sub-Gum Shrimp with Sweet-and-Sour Yak. Nothing else will do. Your stomach has declared it a nonnegotiable issue. It's imperative that the group decides on Chinese, but you must keep the illusion of good faith negotiations.

Solution

You suggest a fair and democratic solution. Everyone jots down what he or she wants for lunch on separate Post-its. Joe wants deli, Susan wants tofu, Harry wants the fish fillet, Janet wants fondue, Harry wants fruit salad. Great. After all the suggestions are written, all the ballots are dropped into a manila envelope. You shake them up, then call in a trustworthy impartial judge . . . such as your secretary. She closes her eyes, reaches in the envelope, and pulls out one Post-it. Your stomach growls with delight—it's the Chinese food. Are you a lucky guy or what?

Astonishing Secret

When you're ready to "negotiate" lunch, peel off a Post-it for each participant to write down their lunch suggestion. Put the Post-it in front of each person *sticky side up*, where each person writes his lunch suggestion. The participants fold their Post-its in half so the sticky side seals the ballot, and the ballots are dropped into the envelope.

The sneaky part happens with *your* Post-it: You still have the Post-it pad. While everybody else is busy writing their suggestions, you write "Chinese" on the top sheet of the pad.

Fold this top sheet in half and then peel it off the pad. Your folded "choice" looks just like everyone else's sealed ballot, except the sticky stuff is on the *outside*. Now, when you innocently place your "sealed" ballot in the envelope, instead of letting it fall to the bottom with the others, *you secretly stick it to the inside wall of the envelope.* No one will ever know.

Show both hands empty as you fairly shake the envelope of secret ballots. Call in your impartial trustworthy secretary, have her reach inside and pick out a "random" Post-it—the very same impartial trustworthy secretary whom you previously instructed to pick out the *Post-it stuck on the inside of the envelope.* Nothing could be fairer. Which isn't quite true, but I'm sure you'll deal with it.

Have her let someone else unfold the randomly selected secret ballot to reveal that you're all having Chinese.

Troubleshooter

Question: What if my stuck Post-it unsticks when I shake the envelope?

Answer: It won't unstick so long as you refrain from shaking the envelope very hard. A gentle "tossed salad" shake is more than enough to be convincing, but if it still unsticks, your secretary can locate the loose Post-it by touch, by feeling for the one sticky Post-it.

Question: Does this negotiating tool have any other applications?

Answer: Sure it does. What movie to see, what color to paint the office, who to hire or fire—anytime you have a variety of opinions and you have to be diplomatic. The Post-it ploy will always do the job.

Question: What if my secretary is out to lunch? Can someone else do it?

Answer: Sure, let any impartial associate in on the secret and let him or her pick the Post-it—or put on an innocent face and do it yourself.

MEMO

The Good Faith Negotiation Neutralizer

1. Place a sticky-side up Post-it in front of each of your fellow negotiators—have each write in his lunch choice. You write in your choice directly onto the top sheet of the Post-it pad.

2. Gather up each Post-it by folding it in half so the sticky stuff seals the writing inside. Drop these secret ballots into the empty manila envelope.

3. Before you drop in your choice, fold the Post-it in half while it's still on the pad, so the sticky side stays on the outside. Peel your "sealed" ballot off the pad and as you place it in the envelope secretly stick it against the inside envelope wall.

4. Give the envelope a quick shake to shuffle the Post-its. Call your secretary. Have her close her eyes, and make sure she shows her hand empty first, then have her reach inside the envelope and pull out your stuck Post-it as a "random selection."

The Forget-Me-Not
Business Card Handout #4—
The Russian Roulette Salary Negotiator

In any negotiation, whenever possible, offer alternatives. Don't back someone into a corner with an all-or-nothing proposition, because they have only one way out. And they'll come out punching. Here's an alternate way to negotiate a raise . . . sort of.

Problem

You're deadlocked over the raise you know you deserve. Your boss doesn't understand why you can't get by on ninety bucks a week like he did when he was your age—in 1953. You counter that you spend ninety bucks a week just on shoe shines so you can look respectable when you pound the pavement looking for more clients for his underfunded business. The boss counters that if you handed out more of your business cards you'd have more clients and wouldn't have to spend so much extra money on shoe shines. That one shuts you up. You know he's right. But you still need to talk him into giving you a raise. It's time to do something gutsy. You think about the last time you did something gutsy . . . you'd rather not think about it.

Solution

Bring out six of your little cardboard salesmen and explain that five of your business cards have "50% cut" written on the back and only one of the cards has "50% raise" written on it. You propose a gutsy game of Salary Roulette with the cards. You have *one* chance of doubling your salary, and *five* chances of losing half your salary.

Your boss brings out his calculator and carefully figures the odds. It's within his boundaries of fair play. He accepts the bet. You deal out the six marked cards facedown on the table. You ask the boss to name any number from one to six. It's his option—any number he wants. The boss scrutinizes the cards, changes his mind numerous times, negotiates with himself, has a quiet moment of prayer, and finally selects the number four. You count to the fourth business card, the boss turns it over, the message on the back of the card says "50% raise." The boss lets loose a tortured yelp. You laugh in his face.

Astonishing Secret

You use your finely honed negotiating skills to always end up at the "50% raise" card—no matter what number the boss names. "Gee, I didn't know I was that good." Don't talk like that. If you don't believe in yourself, who will? Now go out there and get six business cards. On the back of *five* cards write "50% cut." On the back of *one* card write "50% raise."

When You're Ready to Be Astonishing Bring out the six marked cards and deal them into a row printed side up, so that the "50% raise" is the third card from the left or the fourth card from the right—whatever is more convenient for you. With the "50% raise" card in this position you can always either *count* to it or *spell* to it depending on the number called, using one card for each letter or number.

Let's try it.

One:	*Spell* o-n-e from the left.
Two:	*Spell* t-w-o from the left.
Three:	*Count* 1-2-3 from the left.
Four:	*Count* 1-2-3-4 from the right.
Five:	*Spell* f-i-v-e from the right.
Six:	*Spell* s-i-x from the left.

Practice counting and spelling the numbers until it becomes automatic.

You don't have to remember all the combinations. Just look at the cards and say to yourself, "Hmm . . . can I use a number to *count* to the card from the left or right?" If not I'll know I can *spell* the card from the left or right.

You should *pretend* that you always count the cards this way. In astonishment and negotiations proper attitude is ninety-nine percent of the battle.

After you count to the boss's freely selected card flip over the other five cards to reveal they all say "50% cut." Then let the boss flip his carefully selected business card. Resist the temptation to go for double or nothing.

Troubleshooter

Question: Can I use this as yet another novel way to hand out personalized business cards to my clients?

Answer: Of course. Just write "Hi, George" on one card and leave the others blank. Have George turn over his selected card so he can say hello to himself.

Question: What if George wants to see it again?

Answer: You can repeat this mini-amazer up to six times. Although if George continues to be astonished each and every time, you may question his analytical abilities.

MEMO

Russian Roulette Salary Negotiator

1. Write "50% cut" on the back of *five* of your business cards, and "50% raise" on the back of *one* of your cards.
2. Arrange the six marked cards on the table printed side up so the "50% raise" card is third from your left.
3. Ask the boss to name any number from one to six.
4. Figure out which end to start from, and *count* or *spell* to the "50% raise" card.
5. Laugh in his face.

The Astonishing Executive's Official Portable Pocket Negotiator

Before any negotiations begin, put yourself in your opposition's shoes. Argue from their point of view. Role play with an associate. Know at which point you'd be willing to walk away. View the negotiations as a game and remember, he who cares less, wins. And for those negotiations you just have to win, make sure you have your Portable Pocket Negotiator.

Problem

You're in a tense, tough negotiation. Your self-confidence is at a peak—thanks to listening to the audio version of *The Little Engine that Could*.

But you are running out of steam, and the negotiations are falling apart. The ruthless donut lady won't give an inch. She won't refund your money for a stale prune danish.

Solution

Perhaps you shouldn't have left the danish on your desk overnight. But that's not the point. You honor's at stake. You have no choice. That's right—you have to use your Official Portable Pocket Negotiator!

You reach into your vest pocket and whip out what appears to be a simple circle of cardboard printed with pictures of *ten different playing cards*. Just enough cards to play a *single round of poker*.

You make the ruthless donut lady an exceptionally fair proposition: Each of you will randomly select five of the printed playing cards. Whichever one of you ends up with the *winning* poker hand will win the negotiation. And to be ridiculously fair, you'll even *let her* pick out *your* five-card poker hand!

Life doesn't get much fairer than that, so the ruthless yet savvy donut lady accepts the bet.

To select your five-card poker hand she turns the circle of printed playing cards over so she can only see the *backs of the playing cards*. She then takes five ordinary paper clips and clips the backs of five facedown cards. One clip for each of your cards. She has a completely free choice of which five cards she clips for you.

The poker hands have been "dealt." The paper-clipped cards are your hand. The unclipped cards are the donut lady's hand. You haven't touched a thing. And yet, when the circle of printed cards is turned faceup *your* poker hand of five clipped cards turns out to be the *winning hand!*

You softly chuckle as you cash in your prune danish, pop the printed "round o'poker" back into your pocket, and head for the office, confident that you can negotiate your way out of any mess so long as you've got your Official Portable Pocket Negotiator.

The Hard-to-Believe Secret of the Official Portable Pocket Negotiator

Any five facedown cards that are paper-clipped will *always be the winning poker hand.* Yes, you read it right. You take five paper clips and clip them on *any* five facedown cards. You can even change your mind and move a clip to the back of another card—it doesn't make any difference. When the circle of printed cards is turned face up, the paper-clipped poker hand will always be the higher five cards. This will happen every time you try it—over and over again—you couldn't lose even if you tried.

"That's . . . that's impossible." No. Not impossible. Merely astonishing.

How to Construct Your Very Own Official Portable Pocket Negotiator Copy the two sets of printed-card circles so that you have a circle of faceup cards (Figure 5–1) and a circle of facedown cards (Figure 5–2). Use scissors to trim away the extra stuff, leaving you with two circles of paper.

Cut out *one* circle of cardboard the same size as the card circles. (The cardboard from the back of someone else's legal pad is ideal.)

Carefully glue the two sets of card circles to both sides of the cardboard circle—*make extra sure that the dot on each card circle lines up with the other dot. If the two dots don't line up you could be eating stale prune danish.*

Negotiating with the Official Portable Pocket Negotiator Find someone with something that you want. Hand him the "portable pocket negotiator" and let him check it out so he can see there's nothing tricky.

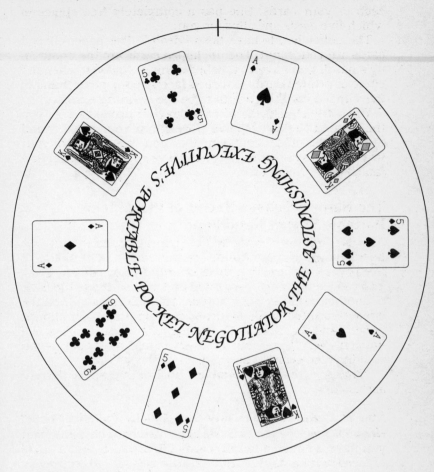

Figure 5-1

Hand him five paper clips and explain that you are going to play one round of poker. Highest hand wins. To be extra fair, you're going to let him pick out your hand by letting him clip any five facedown cards. The five facedown cards he clips will be your poker hand. The remaining unclipped cards will be his poker hand. Make sure he understands that the facedown cards he paper clips will be *your* hand.

After he clips any five facedown cards, let him turn the circle over to discover who has the higher hand.

Try to look surprised when you win. Take your winnings and leave the room as quickly as possible.

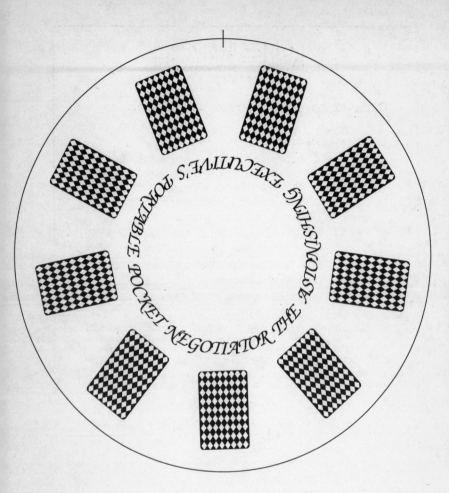

Figure 5-2

Troubleshooter

Question: What if someone clips the five facedown cards and it's not the winning hand?

Answer: Wow, now *that's* close to impossible. Any five facedown cards clipped will always clip the winning hand. Just make sure the clips are clipped while the cards backs are showing, and check to make sure you followed the construction instructions so the two dots line up with each other.

MEMO

Official Portable Pocket Negotiator

1. Copy card circles.
2. Cut out the two card circles and glue them to a circle of cardboard cut from the back of a legal pad so that the facedown cards are on one side and the faceup cards are on the other side. *Make sure the dots match up.*
3. Give five paper clips to your opponent and tell him that to be extra fair you'll let him pick your poker hand by having him clip any five facedown cards.
4. Turn the card circle over to the faceup side, and collect your winnings.
5. Keep the pocket negotiator out of the hands of children, TV evangelists, and IRS agents.
6. When feeling insecure, listen to *The Little Engine that Could.*

Bridge Burner #3—
The Ultra-Persuasive High-Pressure
Heartbreaker

When negotiations get heated and emotional, respond with anything but what you feel. Ask for a glass of water, go to the bathroom, do anything to slow them down. But if your opponent won't give you any breathing room you may be forced to do something out of the ordinary to change the pace.

Problem

Your client is not in a "win-win" mood. He's not even in an "I win and you sorta break even" mood. He wants all the marbles—the marble bag, the dirt you're playing on, and any ancillary marbles you or your loved ones may have acquired. He refuses to compromise. The negotiations are at a standstill.

Solution

You nod your head in resignation, then let out a little cough and comment you're under a lot of stress. You anxiously pat your heart and ask him to feel your pulse. A look of panic comes over his face. *He can't feel your pulse. It's stopped.* Nothing—nada—zip. So far as he can tell you've ceased to function.

While gasping for air you make one last honorable attempt to negotiate. He wouldn't mind killing the deal but this is a bit more than he can handle before dinner. He caves in and accepts your offer.

You slump to the floor, thank him for his kindness, then somehow find the strength to thump your chest to kickstart your heart. *Your pulse suddenly comes back.* He feels good because he doesn't have to explain away a dead exec. You feel good because you'll make your five o'clock squash game.

Astonishing Secret

It's Okay, you can relax, your critical body functions are never at risk. Feel better? Good. I worry about you. Here—have a bread stick.

The nifty secret of this subtle yet highly effective negotiating technique is safely accomplished by applying pressure to an artery that supplies your pulse. So you can stop or start your pulse at will. You can create the illusion of being almost dead whenever it's convenient. Yes, I know . . . your boss has been doing it for years.

To Amuse Your Clients with a Near-Death Experience   Get hold of a small ball or a ball-like object—or even a scrunched up handkerchief tied into knots. Wait until no one is looking, and jam the ball directly up against your bare armpit and hold it there. How do you like it so far? I bet you never dreamed that negotiations could be this much fun.

Keep the ball in place with light arm pressure, then direct your client to feel for the pulse in your wrist (the ball-in-the-armpit wrist). The best way to feel a wrist pulse is with the fingertips, *not* thumb tip. The client feels a strong steady pulse, until you firmly squeeze the hidden ball with your arm. *The pulse taker will suddenly feel your pulse stop.* Twitch your chest, stare blankly into space, and then don't move a muscle (this gets a very strong reaction). After he's caved into your demands thump your other hand against your chest to "jump start" your heart. Relax your arm pressure against the ball, secretly letting the ball drop inside your tucked-in shirt. Reassure your client that you'll probably be Okay.

Troubleshooter

Question: My pulse didn't stop. Why is this?

Answer: Positions of people's arteries vary. Experiment with a larger ball and/or more pressure.

Question: What if I don't have a ball-like object available, but I still want to stop my pulse?

Answer: It's tricky but possible. Lean over a chair back so that the top of the chair presses against your armpit. This technique takes some finesse but it can be done.

MEMO

Ultra-Persuasive High-Pressure Heartbreaker

1. When no one is looking put a ball or ball-like object against your bare armpit. Hold ball in place with light pressure.
2. Have the client feel your wrist pulse using his fingertips.
3. Increase your arm pressure against the ball to stop your pulse.
4. Freeze—don't move a muscle—pretend all body functions have ceased.
5. Thump your chest with your other hand to "jump start" your heart.
6. Relax your arm pressure to restart your pulse.
7. Don't forget your squash racket.

GASP FACTOR

Dissolves Tension

At the moment of astonishment, the client's mind drops all tension and stress to deal with the paradox you've just created. You've substituted a fun problem for the stressful one.

This change of focus creates a mini-vacation for the client's mind, and makes for a relaxed fresh start on the more serious and complicated issues.

6

The Astonishing Trade Show and Hospitality Suite

The Flash-of-Interest Trade Show Stopper

Too often company reps look at the trade show as a monotonous and mandatory obligation. And sometimes it is. Yet letting potential prospects walk in and out is just plain bad business. Training in policies and procedures should be given to every rep on how to attract and deal with potential trade show clients.

Problem

You're all by your lonesome self at the trade show booth and you can't get anyone to stop. You've tried smiling, waving, nodding knowingly, saying, "Hi, how's it going?," cracking your knuckles into the sound system, and handing out tote bags that you acquired from someone else's booth. But no one stops.

You've got a great product, but the zombied-out attendees are numb from the endless avalanche of hype. Their brains are on fluff 'n' fold. They no longer react to normal sensory stimuli.

The only way to break through the fog and grab their attention is with a focused moment of confoundment. You kick yourself for not hiring a professional trade show corporate astonisher. Now you'll have to do it yourself.

Solution

You create a flash of interest by holding a single flash cube at your fingertips. No camera—just an unattached flash cube. When a prospect walks by your booth you hold up the flash cube, say "Smile," then flash the flash cube. The unattached flash cube actually flashes all by itself—right in your fingers! The passerby stops passing. He's interested in how you made the flash cube go off. You leverage his interest into a demo of your product. Other attendees stop by to see what the first one stopped for. Reps from other booths come over to complain that your crowd is blocking the aisle . . . somehow you'll deal with it.

Astonishing Secret

A little-known flash cube phenomenon enables you to set off a flash cube in your bare hands without any outside source of power—just your own wonderful self.

Preparation Buy a box of disposable flash cubes—the kind that flash four times (Figure 6-1). There is a trend toward flash bars, which are a bunch of flash cubes glued together. Do not be talked into buying these. You want the good old-fashioned four-flash flash cube.

Figure 6-1

Get a few pencils and use sharp scissors to cut off a wedge of each pencil eraser (Figure 6-2).

Now look at the bottom of one of your flash cubes (Figure 6-3). You'll see four circular slots. Crossing the middle of each slot is a hair-thin piece of wire. There are a bunch of other holes and stuff down there, but all you care about are the curved slots with the wire. It may take you a moment to see the wire, but it is there—go ahead, I'll wait.

See it? Great. This little wire triggers the flash—anything pressed against one of these wires will cause the flash cube to go off.

"Hey, that's neat. How come no one ever told me this before?" There's a conspiracy to keep executive astonishment in the hands of a select few.

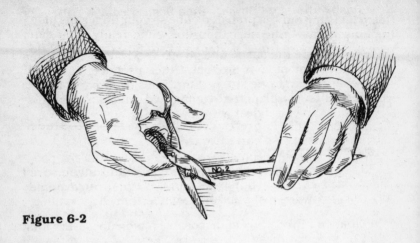

Figure 6-2

Figure 6-3

Okay now, pick up the wedges of eraser and gently insert one into each of the four slots. If the piece of eraser won't fit, trim it down to size with the scissors, then jam it in.

If, upon jamming in the eraser, you notice a flash of white light burned into your retina, that means you jammed in the eraser just a smidgen too far.

So that's it. The slice of eraser should be jammed into the slot deep enough to stay in place, but not so deep that the flash is triggered. I know you figured this out for yourself, but I felt one of us should say it out loud.

Doing It Bring out the prepared cube so your fingertips hide the eraser, say "Cheese," then fire when ready. You can repeat three more times if you want; to be extra flashy do one cube in each hand.

Troubleshooter

Question: This is pretty neat, but I never go to trade shows, where else can I use this?

Answer: Basically anywhere you're competing for people's attention. Start a meeting off with it to make sure everyone is focused and paying attention. Having trouble in a restaurant getting service, take a flash of the waiter. A flash cube can go wherever you go, and it's always ready.

MEMO

Flash-of-Interest Trade Show Stopper

1. Jam a wedge of eraser into one of the four slots of a new flash cube.
2. Bring out the flash cube so your fingers cover the eraser.
3. Say "Smile," then press the eraser with your finger.
4. Wait for your normal vision to return. Next time try to remember to look away when the flash goes off.

The Unforgettable Soda-and-a-Smile Hospitality Suite Surprise

The purpose of a hospitality suite is to thank clients for their support and let prospective clients know the personal side of your company.

The suite is not a "warm-up" for all the reps before the evening begins. If you are going to have a hospitality suite, give the people who come by the attention they deserve. Make it an experience they'll talk about and remember— add a little astonishment.

Problem

You're one of a hundred hospitality suites competing for the attention of a few key clients.

One of the chosen few pops in, munching a cold miniature egg roll from his last stop. He grabs a handful of novelty hors d'oeuvres and a pocketful of peanuts. Bunnylike quick you say, "Hi, how's it going?" But he's already gone— over to the next suite to sample their free goodies.

It feels sort of like Trick or Treat. You've had a fun time dressing up, but you wish you had a trick to make your treats stand out as an unforgettable hospitality suite experience.

Solution

Offer the thirsty client a soda, then suddenly discover that all you have left is an open empty soda can. The client doesn't consider this a peak hospitality suite moment, until you amazingly transform the open soda can into an *unopened* soda can. *Zap!* The can's once-opened hole is now a sealed pull tab. The client pops the pull tab to discover a *full can of soda!* The stunned client takes a sip and stays to chat about your impressive soda skills. You steer the conversation to your impressive product. He burps with delight.

Astonishing Secret

A fake portable hole is used to disguise a full unopened can of soda as empty. This incredible illusion was engineered by California's creative corporate genius John Kennedy.

To create your portable hole cut a piece of shiny black

Figure 6-4

paper (the gloss paper from annual reports looks great) the same size as the punch-out hole on the can. Trash the rest of the annual report, and position the portable hole on top of the punch-out spot by tucking its end under the pull tab (Figure 6–4). For the final artistic touch sprinkle one or two drops of soda from another can around the rim of the disguised can. Now step back a few feet, turn around, and try to imagine that you've never heard about portable holes or disguised soda cans.

Wait a few seconds, and casually glance at the can. It should now look like an empty can. If you can't shift your belief system, call in your secretary and ask her if she sees an empty soda can in the room. She'll say yes, give you a funny look, and leave as quickly as possible. If by chance she says no, I don't see an empty soda can but I do see a full can with a piece of annual report stuck over the punch-out hole, then you've got one sharp secretary. Give her a raise and let her run the business for you. Get a cabin in the woods, a fax, a computer, and a dog named Blue. Check in every now and then and let her know you care.

When You're Ready to Be Astonishing   Casually put the prepared "empty" soda can on a nearby table or chair, so the thirsty client can't help but to see it.

Offer the client a drink. When he says yes, get up and rummage around the room in search of a soft drink, mutter under your breath that you were sure there was a can left. Then go back to your client and say, "No problem . . . we'll improvise."

Write the client's name on a Post-it. Peel off the Post-it and stick it directly onto the portable hole (Figure 6–5). Note that the sticky part is completely stuck against the portable hole. Wait a magical moment—then peel off the Post-it to reveal the instant transformation of the empty into a sealed full can of soda. Drop the guilty Post-it with the secret "hole" into the trash, pop open the can, and give the client a soda and a smile. Be prepared to be unforgettable.

Troubleshooter

Question: It still doesn't look like an empty can to me.

Answer: It's sometimes hard to see the illusion when you know how it's done. Make your portable hole from a different piece of black paper. Experiment with all sorts of different shades and textures until the can of soda gets warm. This is your signal to stop. Whatever portable hole you have on the can will look perfect to anyone just walking in—except maybe your secretary.

Figure 6-5

MEMO

Soda-and-a-Smile Surprise

1. Get a full unopened can of soda.
2. Cut out a black "portable hole" and position it under the pull tab—on top of the punch-out hole.
3. Sprinkle one or two drops of real soda around the rim of the "empty" can. Leave the disguised can on the table until you're ready to astonish.
4. Write the client's name on the Post-it (or any appropriate mystical word). Take the Post-it back from him and stick the Post-it onto the portable hole so that the hole is completely covered by the sticky part of the Post-it.
5. Slide away the Post-it to reveal the new can of soda.
6. Drop the Post-it with its secretly stuck hole into the trash.
7. Get a cabin in the woods, a fax, a computer, and a dog named Blue.

Bridge Burner #4—
The Trade Show Traitor Lost-Wallet Ploy

Competition. Everyone's got it. If you don't, you will. How you deal with your competition says a lot about you. Deal with them fairly, honestly, and as Mom used to say, "If you don't have something nice to say . . ." However, if they play unfairly . . .

Problem

While dozing at your trade show booth an unusually hot prospect walks in. He's ready to buy. Not only that, he's pretty darn educated about the product. He knows the new model has nine equalizers, which reduces the high-density intake while mobilizing and maintaining the OPGs. He even knows that it's soon going to be available in a cherry ash, birch, or oak casing. But he's got just a few more questions. You don't want one like this to get away.

You suggest that the two of you have a drink at the hospitality suite followed by a nice dinner "Where we can put the final touches on the deal."

Everything is going fine at the suite until you realize he's asking some pretty technical questions and pumping you for information on your manufacturing facilities. Wait, this is no prospect, he's a competitor!

Solution

Keep your cool and take him to an obscenely expensive restaurant to discuss "some other projects the company has on the drawing board." After the meal, the check arrives— you've set a new house record for most money spent for a single dinner. The waiters applaud, the owner comes over and gives you a big, big hug. And now for the moment you've been waiting for, having competitor flambé for dessert.

Secretly drop your wallet on the floor near your competitor's chair. Discover the "lost wallet" and offer it to him. He'll say "but it's not mine." Tell your new pal to wave his hand when you point him out to the maître d' so the maître d' will know exactly where the wallet had been found.

You go up to the maître d', thank him for a wonderful meal, and tell him your friend insists on paying for it. Point to your generous friend—he'll enthusiastically wave to the maître d'. Smile, wave back, and leave.

You've created a memorable event for your competitor that he'll talk about and remember for a long time, especially when he has to hand in his expense report.

GASP FACTOR

Unforgettable Proposals

Astonishment by its very nature is memorable. So any proposal, product, or person connected to a moment of astonishment will be talked about and remembered.

7

The Astonishing Sales Meeting

The Wacky Want-Ad Business Projection

If you are trying to forecast the future make sure you can back it up with solid research and statistics, or better yet develop a plan to control the future event to minimize the guesswork.

Problem

You're up at the podium with a conglomerate pie graph of all other pie graphs that you slice up to make all sorts of predictions. You predict a fifteen percent increase in sales and a twenty percent increase in productivity. You predict that stocks will go up, pie graphs will go down, and research will finally discover development.

In general, you predict that everyone in the room will be projectably more solvent if they'll just pay attention to your predictions. Someone says, "Excuse me, oh great one, but how do we know your predictions will come true?" You humorously reply, "Because I said so." Ha ha ha. No one else laughs. You then accurately project a thirty-seven percent decrease in your credibility.

Solution

To prove your business prediction prowess, bring out an envelope and state that it contains your secret prediction. A prediction of an unforeseen event that will happen at this very sales meeting. You bring out a long cut-out single strip of newspaper want ads. You then bring out a pair of scissors and hold them next to the long strip of ads (Figure 7–1) and move the scissors up and down the ad strip. A skeptical audience member decides which spot on the strip to cut,

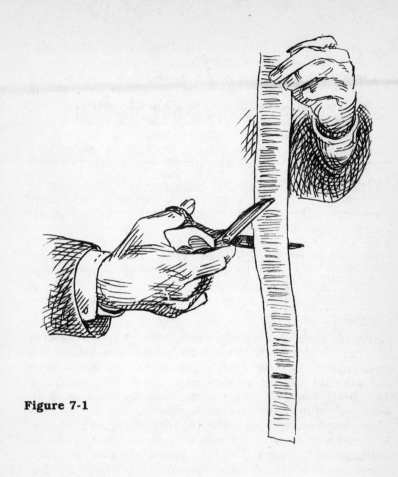

Figure 7-1

then reads the cut-out want ad. You open the sealed prediction envelope and bring out a large folded sheet of paper. Written on it in large letters is the exact same ad that was randomly cut out. Next time you make a business prediction . . . they'll believe.

Astonishing Secret
A bluff based on the fact that a strip of upside down want ads looks just like a strip of right-side up want ads when viewed from a few feet away.

Before You Start Scan the want ads for a "good one" at the *top* of a column. Use your borderline good taste in selecting an appropriate ad. If you can, find an ad that ties in with what you are going to speak about.

Cut out the entire single column of ads so your selected ad is on top. Make sure there is no blank margin on the top or bottom. Use a marker to copy a few succinct lines from the ad onto a large sheet of paper, fold it, and put it in an envelope—and you're all set to predict.

Note: If there are other ads on the *back* of the column, run a line down the full length with your marker to "cancel" out that side.

Trial Run Give the ad column to a trusted someone who won't be at the sales meeting. Now tell them to take the ad strip and hold it upside down. Take a few steps back and look at the ad column. Can you tell if it's upside down or right side up? What do you see? Just a bunch of neutral newsprint. That's exactly what your audience will see—just a bunch of neutral newsprint—and with the slightest encouragement from you they'll believe it's right side up.

Doing It Mention that you made a secret prediction. Pull out the envelope and place it in full sight, at the edge of the stage or taped onto the podium. Then bring out the ad column and hold it *upside down* so that the selected ad is at the *bottom*. As you've already discovered, this upside down condition is impossible to detect. Okay, the meeting audience assumes you have a normal right-side up ad column. Don't say, "I have a normal right-side up ad column." Just be yourself and the crowd will assume this on its own.

Hold the upside down strip so it hangs from your fingertips—while your other hand grabs a big pair of scissors and holds them open in the "about-to-snip" position next to the ad strip (Figure 7–2).

Slowly move the open scissors up and down the strip until someone from the audience tells you where to stop—higher? lower? Give them a chance to change their minds. Sell the point that he selected the exact spot where to cut, then do the deed—snip the strip—and let the lower cut-off portion fall onto the stage floor. Put the scissors and leftover ads from your hand aside. Say, "I don't even want to touch the piece on the floor." Direct someone to pick up the cut-off portion from the floor, and to *read out loud the first ad of the cut-off portion.*

Whoever picks up the strip will naturally turn it *right side*

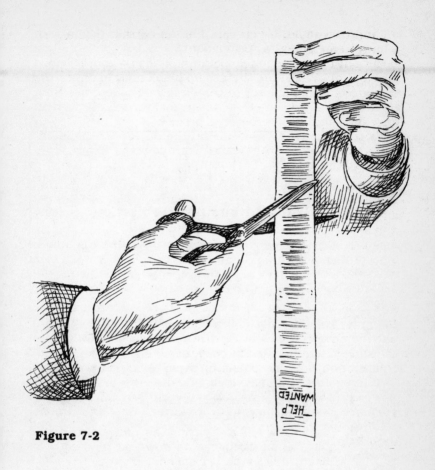

Figure 7-2

up to read it. You're home free. Open your envelope and hold your prediction high—so everyone can read it—as your volunteer reads the ad.

Take a bow and quietly whisper, "I like myself, I like myself."

Troubleshooter

Question: **What if I can't find an appropriate ad at the top of the column?**

Answer: Find an ad you like somewhere *near* the top— then trim off the top of the column so your ad becomes the top ad.

Question: What if the person who picks up the strip reads the wrong ad?

Answer: That won't happen if you give him the correct instructions. Your key line is "Please read the ad at the top where *you* told me to cut."

MEMO

Wacky Want-Ad Business Projection

1. Locate an interesting want ad at the *top* of an ad column, and cut out the entire column so you have one long strip of ads with the selected want ad on top.

2. If there are ads on the back of the strip "cancel out" the back by drawing a long line down the length of the strip with a marker.

3. Use a marker to copy a few lines of the ad onto a large sheet of paper. Fold it up and place in an envelope.

4. *Doing it:* Put your secret prediction envelope in full view of the audience.

5. Stand a few feet away from the audience and hold the ad strip *upside down* so the predicted ad is at the *bottom end*.

6. Move open scissors up and down the strip and cut at freely selected spot.

7. Let cut-off bottom of strip fall to floor.

8. Tell someone to pick up the cut-off section and read the first ad at the cut-off point.

9. Reveal that your secret prediction matches.

10. Find the guy who questioned your business prediction prowess in the first place and give him the want ads and see if he can predict what his next job will be.

The Puncture-Proof Attention Getter

The meat of most meetings can usually be communicated in half the time. Save the details for breakout groups. And whenever you can, use a visual aid to get your point across.

Problem

After three days of corporate mush, no one is listening to your presentation. You test their attention span by saying things like "This is an extremely critical issue that could possibly result in the lower half of your body turning inside out—are there any questions?" The crowd blankly nods as they continue to doodle on the pads in front of them. You continue your carefully crafted presentation and wonder if this is the optimum way to spend your limited time on earth.

Solution

You take a large fully inflated balloon in one hand and a long very sharp needle in your other hand. You hold the sharp point of the needle next to the fully inflated balloon, and slowly push the needle into the balloon.

The balloon doesn't pop. It just sits there—large, fully inflated—with a long sharp needle stuck halfway into it. It's a curious sight. The crowd is no longer comatose. You then remove the needle and pop the balloon—to prove it's real. The wide-awake crowd waits for an explanation. Tell them you just wanted to make sure they were paying attention, and now they will.

Astonishing Secret

Yes—you really can stick a sharp needle into an inflated balloon without popping it. I know it's hard to believe, but then again, so is that tie you're wearing.

Before You Start Blow up a balloon. Then cut out a ¾-inch square of clear scotch tape and stick it firmly onto the inflated balloon next to the neck, where it is tied off (Figure 7–3). Find any long needle-type object. A long thin sharp shish kebab skewer is good because it really shows up, but

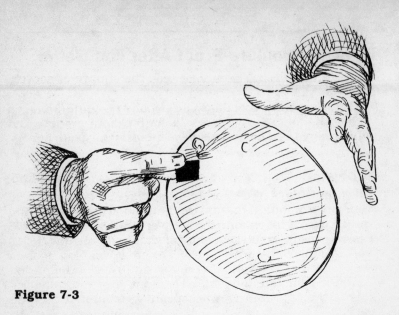

Figure 7-3

a large ordinary sewing needle will work fine too. To make extra sure the skewer or needle slides easily, put Vaseline at the sharp end. Don't ask.

The Hard-to-Believe Theory   When you stick the needle through the scotch tape and into the balloon, the balloon will not pop because the hole is *rigid*, thanks to the scotch tape. So what you have is a slow leak, like a pinhole in an inner tube.

The Experiment   Balloons, like executives, are not created equally. They come in a variety of sizes and thicknesses and react differently to sharp objects. So it's important to test out the type of balloon you plan on puncturing before you make the big presentation. Experiment with rates of inflation and needle sizes to convince yourself that your chosen balloon will survive the assault.

Doing It   Stick the needle into the inflated balloon through the little piece of tape, wait about three seconds for the effect to sink in, then remove the needle and pop the balloon by poking it anywhere on the balloon where the tape isn't. The reason for immediately popping the balloon is to avoid the embarrassment of everyone seeing it slowly deflate. In a meeting, breaking the balloon is also a fine way to signal a coffee break.

Troubleshooter

Question: What if someone sees the square of scotch tape?

Answer: If your audience is a few feet back, they won't.

Question: Do the balloons break often?

Answer: No, just once.

Question: What if my balloon is a genetic mutant and it pops when I poke it through the tape?

Answer: Remark that you just wanted to make sure they were paying attention, then bring out your *second* balloon to demonstrate the real thing.

MEMO

Puncture-Proof Attention Getter

1. Stick a ¾-inch square of clear scotch tape onto an inflated balloon.
2. Poke a sharp needlelike object through the tape and into the balloon.
3. Listen for the oohs and aahs.
4. Remove the needle, and pop the balloon for real.
5. Wonder if this is the optimum way to spend your limited time on earth.

The Vastly Superior New Product Intro

With any new product or service, if there's really a difference, don't just tell them, show them.

Problem

Your new fourteen-hole widget is vastly superior to your old thirteen-hole widget.

Just a few short decades ago they laughed at you for trying to develop a fourteen-hole widget. The experts said it couldn't be done. But here it is—fourteen holes. You've done it. Ha-ha-ha!

But now you need to help the sales staff and clients make the difficult transition. You need a memorable eye-catching way to introduce your vastly superior new product.

Solution

Announce to your sales staff or clients that the old product is out. You highlight this point by displaying the obsolete old product brochure and ripping it to shreds. You fold the discontinued shreds into a compact bundle, say the magic words "Fourteen holes" and unfold the bundle to reveal a torn-no-more completely mended *new* brochure, which introduces your vastly superior new product.

Your sales staff and clients will talk about the nifty things you did with the old product brochure, compelling them to talk about your new product in the same breath.

Astonishing Secret

There's a sneaky way to invisibly switch the old torn brochure for the new torn brochure.

Before You Start   Fold your *new* brochure as follows: Place your new brochure on a table so that the information is upside down. If there were a person across from you, he would be able to read it.

Fold the brochure in half by bringing the end that's closest to you up to the top (Figure 7–4). Fold the halved paper in half again, the same way (Figure 7–5).

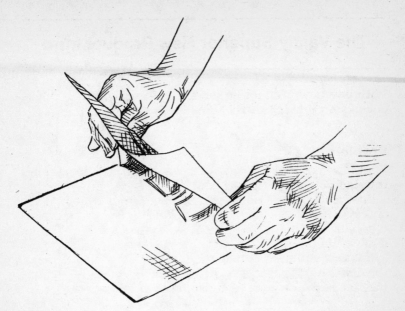

Figure 7-4

Figure 7-5

141

Figure 7-6

Figure 7-7

Figure 7-8

Turn the entire paper over and fold it into thirds by bringing the right side in first (Figure 7–6), followed by the left side (Figure 7–7), squaring it off. Turn the folded square over. You're done folding.

Paint a coat of rubber cement on the square. Then paint a coat of rubber cement, approximately the same size as the square on the back of your old brochure, right in the center.

Let both coats of rubber cement dry and then stick the folded new brochure onto the old brochure so that the flaps open to the left or right (Figure 7–8), *not* up or down.

When You're Ready to Introduce Your Vastly Superior New Product Bring out the old brochure, keeping the folded one hidden at the back. No one will ever guess or think there's a second brochure, so relax and focus on your presentation.

Tear the brochure into three strips (Figure 7–9). Be careful not to tear or inadvertently show the secret folded brochure.

Hold the torn strips together in one column, so that the strip with the hidden folded brochure stays at the back (Figure 7–10). Fold all of the torn strips into a small bundle, so that you have a torn bundle at the front and a folded untorn bundle at the back. Both bundles are approximately the same size.

So far, the about-to-be-astonished crowd has seen you bring out the old brochure, rip it to shreds, and fold it into a small bundle. They sense something special is about to happen.

Figure 7-9

Figure 7-10

143

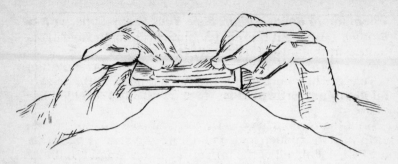

Figure 7-11

Holding the bundle between your hands (Figure 7–11), move the bundle up and down as if to "massage" the pieces back together. As you move the entire bundle up and down, turn the whole thing over so the *untorn bundle* is on top.

That's it! The secret part is done. Unfold the new brochure, careful to keep the hidden torn bundle at the back, to reveal the magical transformation of the old into the new.

Troubleshooter

Question: Why don't the torn pieces fall to the floor?

Answer: Because of the pressure of the folded pieces of the old brochure. If you were to shake the opened new brochure violently up and down the pieces of the old one would fall to the floor. Don't do that.

Question: What if someone wants to see the new brochure? Won't they see the old torn one on the back?

Answer: Start to hand out the new brochure, then stop and say "Let me give you a new one." Put the "restored" brochure in your briefcase or behind the podium, and hand out a new uncreased brochure.

Question: What if I don't have a new product to introduce?

Answer: You can do this to introduce all sorts of changes. Rip up an old contract and transform it into the new one. Rip up the old weekly cafeteria menu, make the new one appear. You can rip up *any* printed information and transform it into the vastly improved version.

MEMO

The Vastly Superior New Product Intro

1. Fold the new brochure or info as instructed.
2. Doing it: Tear the old brochure into three strips, careful to keep the folded brochure concealed.
3. Fold torn strips into a bundle about the same size as the hidden bundle.
4. Turn the bundle over (so new brochure is on top) as you wave it up and down.
5. Unfold new untorn brochure to reveal transformation of new product—carefully keeping the torn bundle at the back.

The Hyper-Efficient Cost Cutter

If your actions aren't consistent with your policies on *all* levels you set yourself up for no one following any of your policies. If you're asking the masses to take mass transit to cut costs, you better not be seen getting into your limo.

Problem

The theme of last year's sales meeting was "Cutting Costs While Maintaining Efficiency." You spared no expense in getting this crucial message across to the troops.

You started the general session with the Royal Scottish Bagpipe Marching Band, followed by a prize session of "objet d'giveaways" including logo-inscribed towels, T-shirts, sunglasses, tote bags, umbrellas, paperweights, ponchos, pens, and pencils.

Finally for the afternoon beach Olympics you flew the entire gang to Greece to hold the athletic contests at the foot of Mount Olympus. Unfortunately you ran out of money before the start of the second day when you were going to discuss the "Cutting Costs While Maintaining Efficiency" part.

As a result of your oversight, the budget for your upcoming sales meeting has been somewhat reduced. You have been allocated a total of nine dollars to come up with an entertaining way to get your cost-cutting message to the crew. You complain about the meager budget. They cut it by another two dollars. This forces you to cancel the "Think and Grow Rich Speaker." Now you're really stuck.

Solution

You display a strip of newspaper tastefully decorated with dollar signs and say, "This strip represents our business costs."

You then display a large pair of scissors and say, "These scissors represent *cost-cutting* measures." Even the gang in the back who were out in the Jacuzzi until 5:00 A.M. understand the message so far.

"Our primary objective is to *cut costs*"—and here you use the cost-cutting scissors to dramatically cut a hunk of dollar signs from the center of the paper strip. You let the cutout dollar signs waft gently to the floor . . . waft . . . waft . . .

waft. So far everyone gets it—you want to cut costs. Everyone else also understands that you've cut the paper strip into two pieces.

"But the real trick is to cut costs and *maintain efficiency*." In your best astonishing executive style, you slowly reveal that the two cut strips of paper are now a single efficient strip of paper. Completely restored!

You cut the paper again and again as you cut production costs, packaging costs, marketing costs. After each scissors cut, the paper dollar signs waft to the floor, yet the efficiency of the single strip of paper is always maintained.

You've cut costs yet maintained efficiency. What's the secret? Just a little rubber cement and talcum powder.

Astonishing Secret

The cut paper automatically glues itself together after each cut. All you have to do is prepare a special strip of glue-o-matic paper, and you'll be ready to unglue your associates whenever you feel the need.

Preparing the Glue-O-Matic Paper   Cut out a long strip of newspaper, about two inches wide and up to two feet long. A shorter strip will work almost as well. You'll just be limited to the number of snips you can make.

Lay the long strip of newspaper flat across the top of your desk and get a bottle of rubber cement, a dark-colored marker, and some talcum or baby powder from the drug store.

Use the marker to draw dollar signs on one side of the strip. Then on the other side, paint a coat of rubber cement. In a few seconds the rubber cement on the paper strip will be dry, but still sticky. Rubber cement never completely dries—that's why it's rubber cement, and that's why this thing works.

Sprinkle a very light layer of powder over the sticky side of the paper and gently rub it over the paper with your fingers. The powder keeps the paper from sticking together when you don't want it to.

Sprinkle a little powder down your shirt—the reward for a job well done—and you're all set to be astonishing.

Doing It   Hold the prepared strip of paper at the top, so the rubber cement surface faces your body. This is the key success factor. The rubber cement surface must be on the inside toward your body, *not* on the outside. The side with the dollar signs is visible to the audience.

The rest is automatic. Fold the paper in half and snip off right below the crease (Figure 7–12). Grab one of the lower ends (Figure 7–13) and gently let the cut strip unfold to reveal a single strip of automatically restored paper! For an instant replay, fold the strip and do it again . . . and again and again and again.

Now just for the fun of it, snip below the crease at a sharp angle (Figure 7–14), and when the strip unfolds you can reveal how you've cut corners (Figure 7–15).

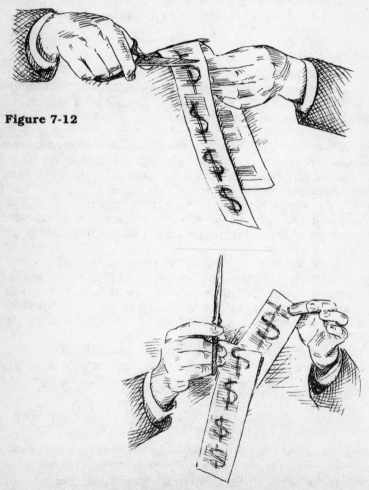

Figure 7-12

Figure 7-13

Figure 7-14

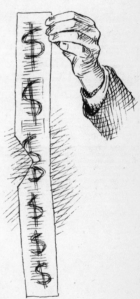

Figure 7-15

Troubleshooter

Question: When I snipped the strip I ended up with two pieces of cut paper. Where did I go wrong?

Answer: The only thing that can go wrong is that you might have put too much powder on the rubber cemented side. A light "dusting" is all that you need.

MEMO

The Hyper-Efficient Cost Cutter

1. Secretly prepare a long strip of newspaper by drawing dollar signs on one side and then coating the other side with a layer of rubber cement.

2. Wait a few seconds for the rubber cement to dry, then lightly sprinkle the talcum powder. Rub the powder evenly over the paper.

3. Hold the prepared strip so the rubber cement surface is on the *inside*, closest to your body.

4. Snip off below the crease with the scissors.

5. Let the restored strip unfold by grabbing one of the lower ends.

6. Refold and repeat over and over and over.

7. Sprinkle some talcum powder down your shirt.

The Undressed-for-Success
Memorable Meeting Inducer

Practice what you preach. If the company is really a family as you've led them to believe, then treat them like family. If you really mean you'll do anything to help increase sales, back it up with something tangible.

Problem

It's the last speech. A few more words of encouragement from the president. A few more discreetly stifled yawns, and the sales meeting is over. Two hundred seventy specially embossed unused note pads and over nine hundred pounds of honey-roasted peanuts are shipped back to the generic sales meeting junkyard. A janitor sweeps out the discarded pie graphs, and it's as though the event never happened. Gee—it's too bad that no one cared enough to create a final astonishing moment that would have made this sales meeting talked about and remembered.

Solution

You close the meeting by telling the troops that you think of them as family. "We'd do anything for you guys. I know it's a cliché, but honest to God, we would really give you the shirt off our back—we sincerely mean that." With tears in your eyes you shake the sales manager's hand, grab his tie, and pull it right through his neck, still tied. Then you grab his shirt collar and yank the shirt right off his back! You comment, "I wasn't kidding; we'll do anything to help you." This vivid image of self-sacrifice leaves the inspired attendees eagerly marking off their calendars in joyous anticipation of the next sales meeting.

Astonishing Secret

The "shirt off the back" guy has been secretly redressed for success, so you can easily rip off his shirt and tie with a minimum of bodily injury.

Redressing for Success Where no one can see you, have your accomplice take off his jacket. Then have him loosen his tie, and without untieing it, slip it over his head. Finally have him take off his shirt. Try to resist the temptation to make embarrassing jokes.

Drape the shirt over his back and button the collar and top two buttons as shown in Figure 7–16.

With sensitivity and tact, gently tuck his tie under his collar by taking the loop above the tie knot and placing half the loop under the right collar and half under the left collar (Figure 7–17).

If the tie slips out from under the collar, grab your handy-dandy hotel emergency sewing kit and run a thread from one side of the collar, around the neck, to the other side of the collar to hold the tie in place.

After the tie is secured under the collar, drape the shirt-sleeves down along his arm and rebutton the cuffs around his wrists (Figure 7–18). Have him put his coat on and button it to hide the secret redress (Figure 7–19). Assure your accomplice he's never looked better.

Figure 7-16   **Figure 7-17**

Figure 7-18

Figure 7-19

When You're Ready to Show Them You Care At the appropriate time during your presentation have your secretly redressed accomplice join you on stage. While saying that you'd do "anything for the gang" your accomplice fiddles with his cuffs and secretly unbuttons them. You'll be fine, the crowd is watching *you* not him.

After repeating that you'd give the shirt off your back, ask your accomplice if he'd be willing to do the same. "Of course," he replies. You say, "Good, I'll do it for you."

Grab his tie at the knot and pull down, freeing the tie. If it's held in place with a thread you'll have to pull a little harder to break the thread.

Immediately take a few steps forward with his loose tie in hand and say, "We'll start with his tie." At the same time your "surprised" accomplice moves his hand up to the top button as if to feel if the tie is really gone.

As you are stepping back to your accomplice, he secretly unbuttons the top two buttons and holds the shirt closed. As you get back to him you put your hand on his shoulder and immediately slide this hand up and grab his collar. Yank the collar straight up and the shirt will appear to go right through his coat, leaving him barechested.

Step forward with his shirt, and after the laughter dies down state, "When we say we'd do anything for you, we mean we'd do anything for you!"

Troubleshooter

Question: How do I top this at my next sales meeting?
Answer: Give me a call—we'll figure out something.

MEMO

Undressed-for-Success
Memorable Meeting Inducer

1. Secretly rig shirt.
2. Secretly rig tie.
3. Put on jacket so the suit looks normal.
4. Doing it: Wait for an appropriate emotional moment, grab the guy's tie, and yank. Grab his shirt collar and yank.

The Forget-Me-Not
Business Card Handout #5—
Breakout Group Boredom Buster

Get your people involved. Ask for their opinions. Put your agenda down and listen to their agenda. The more involved they feel, the more they'll help you achieve your objectives. And if your objective is to have a productive breakout session, you've got to find ways to get them involved from the start.

Problem

You're sitting with your breakout group where you and your fellow breakout groupies have been instructed to brainstorm a marketing plan to distribute 240,000 midget widgets. The future of your company hangs in the balance—not to mention the fate of nearly a quarter million itty-bitty widgets.

The responsibility is overwhelming, but first you have an even larger responsibility. That's right. First you must come up with yet another wildly brilliant way to hand out a few more of your beloved yet undistributed business cards, while at the same time getting the gang revved up.

Editors' Note If you don't take out five business cards right now you'll miss out on one of the most astonishing things in this book.

Astonishing Solution/Secret/Troubleshooter, All Wrapped Up Into One

Blow the dust off five business cards and motivate five members of the breakout group to autograph the back of the cards, so that a different name is on each card. Get them to write their names so they go completely across the card (Figure 7–20). Gather up the five signed cards, turn them over so you can't see the signed names, and mix them up so no one has any idea whose name is where.

Hold your precious cards in a nice neat stack, then rip the stack in half (Figure 7–21). Put *one* torn section on the table so that your *printed* business card side is showing. Put the second torn section on the table so a torn autograph shows (Figure 7–22). Carefully follow the directions to make sure you enjoy the maximum bafflement.

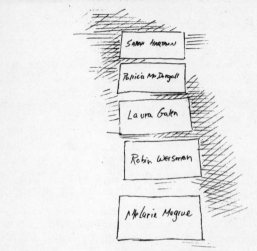

Figure 7-20

Figure 7-21

Figure 7-22

Position Check

Five autographed business cards have been shuffled and stacked into a neat pile. You ripped the entire stack in half (*not* one at a time, but the *whole stack at once*). You put one torn half on the table autograph side *up*, and the other torn half on the table autograph side *down*.

1. The breakout group question of the day is "Will the cards match?"

2. To find the mystical answer, each word of "Will the cards match" must be spelled as follows: One torn piece is moved for each letter. So direct one of your break mates to remove the top piece of *either* stack, and place that piece on the *bottom* of the *same stack*. That first move represents the letter *W* of "Will." Tip: Make sure only *one* piece is moved from the top, and that the one piece goes directly underneath on the bottom of the same stack.

3. The next letter in Will is *i*, so direct someone to move the top piece of *either* stack and place it underneath on the *bottom* of the same stack. The next letter of "Will" is *l*—have another piece moved from the top of *either* stack and placed on the *bottom* of the stack it was moved from.

   The last letter of "Will" is another *l*. Same procedure—*one* piece moved from the *top* of *either* stack and placed on the *bottom* of the *same stack*.

4. The word *Will* has been spelled by the random movement of card pieces in the two stacks. No one could possibly predict which two card pieces will now be in top position. Slide off the *top* piece of each stack (Figure 7–23).

   One piece will show a partial autograph—the autograph on the other piece will be facedown. Do not turn either piece over—leave them exactly as they are, one up and one down. Slide the two pieces in front of the person who wrote the partial autograph.

   Remember to leave the two pieces just as they are—*one faceup and one facedown*. All right, back to the two piles. The next word of "Will the cards match?" is *the*.

   Have someone spell "the" by moving one piece for each letter from the top of either pile, placing each piece on the bottom of the same pile just as you did with the first word, making sure only *one* piece is moved at a time. Since there are three letters in "the," three pieces are moved. And just as before, after spelling the word, carefully slide the new top piece of each pile—keeping one facedown—over to the person who matches the partial autograph.

"Will the cards match?" The next word is *cards.* You know the ritual—spell "cards" by moving one piece for each letter from the top of either pile to the bottom of the same pile. After "cards" has been spelled (don't forget the "s") slide off the two new top pieces and put them in front of their namesake. (Note: the person who moves the pieces has a *completely* free choice of which pile to move the pieces from. He can alternate back and forth or move just one piece from one pile then the rest of the pieces from the other pile—or even move all the pieces from just one pile. He is a free agent. The options are wide open.

5. Two pieces remain in each stack. "Will the cards match?" The last word is *match*—and one last time have someone move one piece for each letter from the *top* of *either* pile to the *bottom* of the *same pile*—until *match* is spelled. Slide the top two pieces to the appropriate person—leaving just two pieces behind. Slide those last two pieces over to their owner.

"Will the cards match?" "Come on—who are you trying to kid? That would be genuinely impossible," unless of course you're an astonishing exec.

Figure 7-23

MEMO

Breakout Group Boredom Buster

1. Get five business cards autographed on the back with five different names.

2. Mix up the five cards so no one knows which name is where.

3. Tear the stack of five cards in half (all at once) and put one torn section on the table, autograph side up. Put the other torn section on the table autograph side down.

4. The magic question is "Will the cards match?" Have someone spell each word by moving one torn piece from the *top* of *either* pile to the *bottom* of the *same pile*. Example: four letters in "will," so four card pieces are moved.

5. After spelling each word, slide off the *top* piece of each pile (one piece is autograph side up, one piece is autograph side down) and put the two pieces in front of their namesake. Be careful not to reveal the hidden half autograph.

6. After "Will the cards match?" is spelled, two torn pieces will remain. Put those last two pieces in front of the appropriate person, and let them discover the boredom-busting miracle. (Note: This can be done for less than five people, simply let whoever you're doing it for write the names of five friends on the back of the five cards and off you go.)

Bridge Burner #5—
The Sound of No Hands Clapping
Presentation Meditation

When rehearsing your presentation, remember that the actual presentation will take about twenty-five percent longer than you anticipated. Keep it as close to the point as possible, especially for large groups. If the speech is too long, you'll lose the entire message, not just the part that drags.

Problem

Backstage, nervously waiting to give his sales talk, is the man who won the award for dullest presentation given by a person not yet dead. The Crown Prince of Boredom stares curiously at you.

You're sitting at the table, eyes closed, as you slide a quarter across your forehead, down your nose, and onto a paper covered with quarter-size circles. You appear calm, relaxed, tranquil. If it weren't for the hair gel, you could easily be mistaken for a deranged Zen monk. You open your sparkling clear eyes and see the Dean of Dull. He's curious: "What the heck are you doing with that quarter?"

You explain it's a Zen meditation technique. The act of sliding a quarter across your forehead, down your nose, and onto a circle focuses your personal power. It gives you a special charisma that ensures your presentations will be talked about and remembered.

The Yawn Master begs you to teach him.

You give him a clean sheet of paper, a quarter, and a pencil. Direct him to draw quarter-size circles all over the paper using the quarter as a guide.

Tell him to close his eyes, visualize a focused, attentive audience, visualize the circles in his mind, then slide the edge of the quarter across his forehead, slide it down his nose, and drop the quarter onto the paper with the circles. You congratulate him on a good first effort and have him draw a few more circles, close his eyes, visualize a cheering audience, and this time slide the edge of the quarter across his cheek, down his chin, and onto the paper with the circles. You continue to guide him through the personal power meditation until it's time for him to give his presentation.

Funny—he doesn't feel any different. Somewhat skeptical, he goes out and gives his typical boring presentation. But this time a miracle happens—the audience is attentive, focused, hanging on his every word—staring in astonishment at the crisscross pencil streaks across his forehead, down his nose, and over his face.

Yes, the act of using a pencil to draw circles around a quarter left a heavy residue of lead on the quarter's edge, which was then slid across his forehead, down his nose, and over his face, leaving him a marked man. The novelty-starved crowd is just thrilled. The charismatic presenter gives you a thumbs up—you cheer him on—and meditate on how good it feels to live in a country where you can make so many people so happy for just twenty-five cents.

GASP FACTOR

Breaks Down Barriers

A moment of shared amazement breaks down all barriers. You are forced to admit that you have no idea what the heck is going on. You're now all in the same boat, relating to each other as equals. Even if the attention turns to how the trick was accomplished, you're still on equal footing.

8

The Astonishing CEO in Training

Don't-You-Just-Hate-When-That-Happens Pain Predicament

In every aspect of business, there's one surefire rule. Keep a sense of humor. Don't lose your ability to see the absurdity of a situation or the ability to make fun of yourself.

People admire those select few who can laugh at themselves in the face of professional or personal discomfort.

Problem

As a future CEO you must appear impervious to pain. You must develop the knack of making quotable quips during open heart surgery. As CEO you must inspire others to pound themselves into a pulp in the quest for corporate glory and make them sort of like it. Unfortunately just thinking about the word *pain* gives you a jumbo tummy ache and makes you want to curl up on your rest mat.

Solution

When giving dictation to your secretary, emphasize a point by slamming your hand on the desktop—and "accidentally" skewer your hand on the memo spike (Figure 8-1). Wait for your secretary to notice your painful predicament, then give a cheerful little chuckle and say, "Boy—don't you hate when that happens?" Casually unskewer yourself, wipe off the spike, and continue dictating your letter.

Astonishing Secret

While the secretary is engrossed with taking your dictation, slyly switch your normal memo spike for a "special effects"

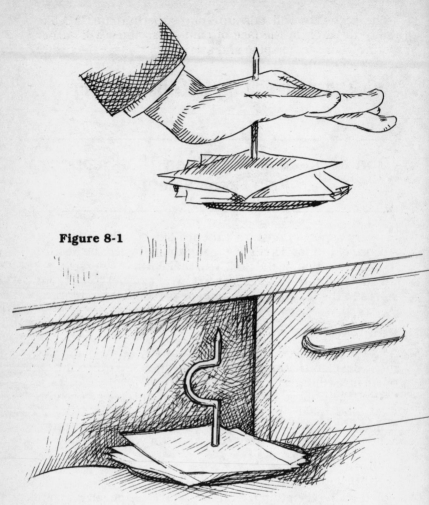

Figure 8-1

Figure 8-2

spike hidden behind your desk (Figure 8–2). Slam your hand on the desk to "make a point" and immediately slide your hand into spiked position (Figure 8–3). Raise the hand with the spike off the desk, draw your secretary's attention to the "amusing incident," then unspike yourself by dropping the hand behind your desk, where your other hand secretly removes the spike, leaves it on the floor, then brings the normal spike out to put on the desk.

The secretary will talk up your superhuman CEO-like ability to laugh in the face of pain—associates will gather around your memo spike and ask you if it's true. Modestly deny everything.

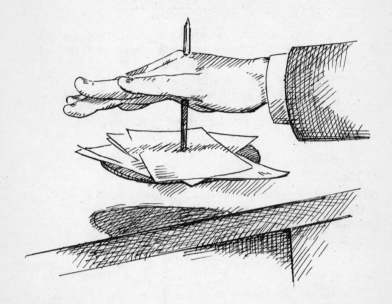

Figure 8-3

The Ten-Heads-Are-Better-Than-One CEO Tiebreaker

People who are successful usually have learned the knack of unleashing their creative powers to see new uses for a product, unique distribution channels, or new venues for communicating a message. They know that when everyone is going through the front door, why not try going through the back door?

The only way to get head and shoulders above the competition is to have the nerve to try something different.

Problem

You want to be talked about and remembered as an exceptionally resourceful exec, so that when the powers-that-be pick the new CEO, your name will stand out as the obvious choice.

Solution

Use your vast resources to obtain fifteen or twenty strategically located seats at a hot "must see" Broadway show. Send some of the tickets to the CEO decision makers, and distribute ten of the tickets to ten *completely bald* theater lovers. Your deal with the ten bald men is that in return for the valuable free tickets, each must paint a letter of your name on top of his bald head, using luminous glow-in-the-dark paint, which you also supply free of charge. *Plus* each luminous lettered bald head must sit in a specific assigned seat—no switching allowed. Your work is done. The show starts. The lights dim. When your CEO decision makers look down from their balcony seats, they'll see vivid proof of your CEO-caliber thinking. The job will be yours.

Bridge Burner #6—
The Just-Sign-Here Instant Approval Kit

Every now and then there's a power-hungry boss who only speaks to you when his coffee isn't hot enough. A pat on the back or even a "good job" would make your week. Unfortunately your boss considers acknowledgment a sign of weakness.

Not to worry. In the long run you'll get the credit that you deserve. And remember, as you climb up the ladder a few encouraging and supportive words to your staff on a regular basis can work wonders.

But until then, why not take the initiative and find ways to congratulate yourself for a job well done?

Problem

There's a memo on your desk from your boss, Mr. Harelick.

TO: Human Resources
FROM: Harley Harelick

Mr. Astonishing Executive has done an outstanding job this year. So when it comes time for his annual review, I want it noted in his file that Mr. Astonishing should be given the absolute *maximum bonus* allowed under corporate policy.

There's only one problem; this wonderful memo from the boss was not written by your boss. It was written by you, just to see what it would look like.

Your boss would eat his foot before signing a memo like that. You desperately search for a sneaky way to get the boss to sign your wonderful memo. You think about disguising his foot as a meat loaf, but something tells you there has to be a better way. . . .

Solution

You get the boss to sign a homemade birthday card for one of your office buddies.

When the boss is out of sight the birthday card magically transforms into your wonderful memo, personally signed and approved by Mr. Harley Harelick himself.

Astonishing Secret

The homemade birthday card is an ingenious scam that covers a trapdoor card. When the birthday card is signed the signature secretly ends up on your wonderful memo. "Huh?" Trust me.

Making the Bogus Trapdoor Birthday Card Get a batch of twenty or thirty blank index cards, lined or unlined in the festive birthday color of your choice. Plain white will do just fine. Take one card and cut off the bottom quarter. Throw away the small piece (Figure 8–4).

Go back to your stack of index cards and write your wonderful memo on the top card, as shown in Figure 8–5. On the three-quarter card write in your birthday message. Legitimately obtain or forge the signatures of your other office mates on the three-quarter birthday card as shown in Figure 8–6. *Note:* Every available space for a signature must be filled. Place the signed three-quarter birthday card on top of the index card stack so it covers your wonderful memo. Slip a reasonably wide rubber band around the stack so the rubber band completely covers the cut-off end of the birthday card. Thanks to this rubber band the top card appears to be a single complete uncut birthday card (Figure 8–7).

When You're Ready to Astonish Grab the rubber-banded stack and a pen, corner your boss, and do a little song and dance about the birthday surprise for your office pal. "The

Figure 8-4

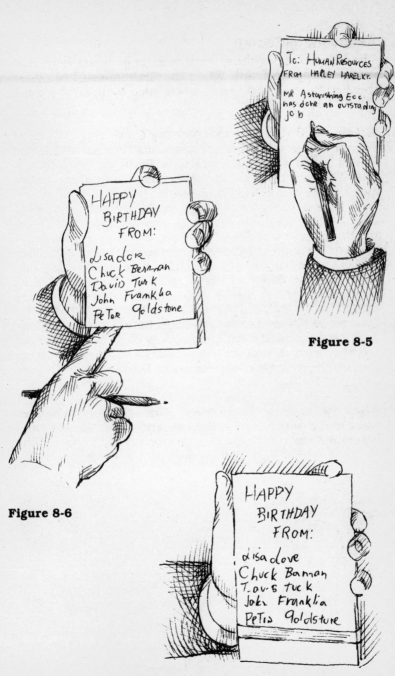

Figure 8-5

Figure 8-6

Figure 8-7

whole gang has signed it." Hang on to the stack of cards, and give him the pen. Tell him to sign in the space below the rubber band (Figure 8–8). "It's all part of the birthday fun, ho-ho-ho."

And that's it. Without knowing it, the boss has just signed your wonderful bonus memo. Walk into your office, close the door, slide out the approved signed memo, and drop it off at Human Resources. Try to wipe that grin off your face.

Figure 8-8

The Just-Sign-Here Disposable Calculator Kit

This version's just for fun—an intriguing mini-amazer to "show off a new invention you've developed." A "disposable calculator." You bring out your revolutionary gadget— it looks just like a stack of blank index cards. You input a math problem into the disposable calculator by writing 365 + 181 on the top card. You explain it's a personal disposable calculator and only works when someone personally signs his name, so you persuade a curious onlooker to sign his name.

You slide out the signed card, wait three seconds, and flip it over. The calculator has worked. The total of 546 has mysteriously printed itself. It can't be and yet it is. Give the disposable calculator card to the signee as a souvenir and let him try to figure out where the batteries go.

Astonishing Secret

It's the good old trapdoor index card gimmick, using numbers instead of birthday cards.

Setup   The rubber band is around the stack. On the top card *above* the rubber band write "365 + 181 = 546" (Figure 8–9). Then cover the numbers with a blank half card (Figure 8–10), and you're all set.

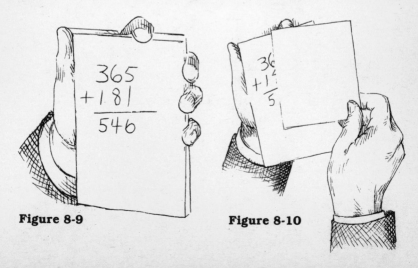

Figure 8-9   **Figure 8-10**

Doing It Bring out the banded blank index cards, and write "365 + 181" (Figure 8–11). Your pal signs his name under the last number (Figure 8–12). Turn the stack over (the signed card is on the bottom), and separate the *signature end* of the bottom card of the stack and slide it out (Figure 8–13). It will look exactly as if you're sliding out the bottom card that you just wrote the numbers and signature on, but the secret three-quarter card stays under the rubber band as the computed card comes out.

Keep *everything* facedown so that none of the writing shows. Put the stack away in your pocket, and drop the number card on the signee's quivering hand. Tell him to turn the card over—to reveal his own signature with the appearance of the astonishing addition.

Troubleshooter

Question: What happens if the three-quarter card falls off during the signing?

Answer: This won't happen because you hold the three-quarter card in place on the stack as the card is signed.

Figure 8-11

Figure 8-12

Figure 8-13

173

MEMO

The Just-Sign-Here Instant Approval Kit

1. Use a stack of index cards to create a bogus birthday card, which conceals your wonderful memo. (See Making the Bogus Trapdoor Birthday Card, page 168.)
2. Approach your boss with the song and dance about a birthday card for an office mate, *which everyone else has signed.*
3. Persuade the boss to sign his name on the one remaining blank spot on the birthday card, which happens to be on the end *below* the rubber band.
4. When the boss is gone, remove your personally signed-by-the-boss memo and drop it off at Human Resources. Or play it safe—frame your personally autographed memo and hang it on the wall.
5. Never sign your name to anything with a rubber band around it.

GASP FACTOR

Lets You Be You

Unlike jokes, mini-amazers can be tailored to fit your personality.

If you're dramatic, be dramatic. If you're funny, be funny. And if you're the sincere, straightforward type, that's fine too. The mini-amazer will create the fun for you.

9

The Astonishing CEO

The Revenge of the Vacuum Cleaner Cards
CEO Indulgence

"Good morning, I'd like to start the day by reminding you of how important I am." You don't hear that very often, but you can tell by some people's actions that that's how they feel.

Nothing turns people off quicker than self-importance, and as soon as there's a power shift, someone, somewhere, will find a way to remind them of how important they used to be.

Problem

You did it. You're top doggy. You've just become CEO "chief executive o'stonisher." You've got it all—the super-deluxe oversized cubicle, the private fax machine with your face painted on it, and your very own built-in vacuum system to keep personal hair balls and dust bunnies under strict security.

But you can't really enjoy yourself until you break the news of the promotion to your old boss George—the guy who once stuck his boot on your desk and said, "Pretend it's an ice cream cone." You rack your brain for just the right way to tell thirty-one-flavors George that the boot is now on the other foot.

Brilliant CEO Solution

For your first official act as CEO take all your undistributed business cards and rip them into a billion bitty pieces. Yes, I know, this is a cathartic moment for all of us.

Now call good old George into your office and tell him

you've discovered a weird thing about your vacuum cleaner. Curious George watches as you cover your desk with a shower of business card flakes. You then point the vacuum cleaner nozzle at the desk, turn the switch to "blow," and the pieces fly off the desk to make a mess on the floor. George views this as a fairly unremarkable event, until he notices that some of the card pieces have stayed on the desk . . . and for some inexplicable reason those leftover pieces have formed the letters *CEO*. George nervously looks up—you humbly shake your head and shyly smile. "Yep, I'm your new boss." You then direct George's attention to the mess on the floor, hand him the vacuum cleaner, and politely and gently say, "It sucks." Quietly leave the office to let George ponder the historical significance of your last words. Peek in every now and then until he's cleaned up the mess.

Astonishing Secret

Tear up all your old business cards into a pile of tiny pieces. This may be more fun than you can stand but try to be strong. Now grab a bottle of rubber cement and paint a thin invisible coat onto your desk top so it spells *CEO*. Wait a few moments for the rubber cement to become tacky—then call in your special buddy to show him a "weird thing you discovered about your executive vacuum cleaner."

Sprinkle your business card confetti so it completely covers the desktop, then bring out Mr. Vacuum Cleaner, switch it on to "blow," and point it at the top of your desk. The loose business card confetti will fly all over the office, except for the pieces stuck to the rubber cement that prophetically spell out *CEO*. Switch the blowing vacuum to its normal suck mode, hand it to your new carpet cleaner, and say something profound like "Nature abhors a vacuum—but then again so do CEOs."

Troubleshooter

Question: That wasn't as profound as I had hoped. Don't you have something more meaningful to leave us with?
Answer: See the next page.

10

The Complete Astonishing Executive

When you first walked into my office you were just another business suit waiting to be wrinkled—now there's a burst of applause at the mere mention of your initials. And, yes, you've even learned not to giggle. All right—I admit it. You've become pretty darn incredible. You've learned to break the ice, get a client's attention, get your proposals talked about and remembered, get *you* talked about and remembered.

One day soon, you'll be in the office, or with a client or with the stockholders, and without even trying you'll just naturally stand out as someone special. Your executive glow of confidence will shine through and you'll be astonishing just by being your wonderful mini-amazing self. That's right. The real secret of executive success has nothing to do with cleverness or diabolical power plays—the real secret comes from the inside. It's not who you know or what you drive or how you dress—it's not about the size of your bank account or the label on your suit—it's not. . . .

"Excuse me."

"Yes?"

"What about a Rolex?"

"What about it?"

"I don't have one."

"You're kidding . . . you don't have a Rolex?"

"Well . . . I was going to buy one, but then I blew the twelve grand on a new pacemaker for Mom. It was a tough call."

"Jeez . . . how can you not have a Rolex? I mean, come on, how do you expect to get anywhere without a Rolex?"

Moms-Come-and-Go-but-a-Rolex-Is-Forever
Ingenious Acquisition Trick

Problem

A frivolous spending spree has left you without the resources to purchase a Rolex. Your astonishing career is at a dead stop. "Gee, where did I go wrong?"

Solution and Secret

Find a Rolex exec and tell him you've marked a secret page number in this book with a paper clip. A secret page number that will exactly match his secret Rolex number. He'll have no idea which secret Rolex number you're talking about. So you show him the chart on page 180 to calculate his secret Rolex number (reproduced here in miniature for your learning convenience).

Figure 10-1

1. Put your finger on any number.
2. Move your finger along the line to the opposite number.
3. Subtract the smaller number from the new larger number.
4. Add *1* to the result.
5. Divide the new number by 2.
6. This result is your secret Rolex number. Remember it.

He is thinking of a secret Rolex number. You've secretly marked the page number in this book with a paper clip. The two numbers are supposed to match, but he knows they can't match because the secret number he is thinking of is $3\frac{1}{2}$, and everyone knows there is no page $3\frac{1}{2}$. He rechecks his calculation—yep, it's $3\frac{1}{2}$. He knows you've blown it. Of course he won't tell you this, he'll just quietly sneer at your upcoming humiliation as his $12,000 Rolex keeps perfect time.

The trap is set. You innocently ask if he'd like to make a small wager that your secret page prediction will match his secret Rolex number. He tries to keep a straight face as he says, "Sure . . . what's the bet?" You say, "Oh, I don't know—let's keep it friendly. Your Rolex for my Toyota."

Sign the necessary documents, imagine how nice the Rolex would look in your sock drawer, take a deep breath, and turn to page $3\frac{1}{2}$ . . . you can thank me later.*

---

*NOTE: So you don't forget, put a paper clip on page $3\frac{1}{2}$ right now. I'd hate to see you lose your Toyota on a technicality.

Figure 10-2

1. Put your finger on any number.
2. Move your finger along the line to the opposite number.
3. Subtract the smaller number from the new larger number.
4. Add *1* to the result.
5. Divide the new number by 2.
6. This result is your secret Rolex number. Remember it.

Well, I guess that about wraps it up.

"Hey, wait a sec."

Now what?

"I want more."

Oh . . . all right. Turn to page 182.

For More Information
on Executive Astonishment Including:

Briefcase Bafflers—A mind boggling collection of pocket-size magical gadgets specially designed for executive astonishment.

Astonishing Executive Video Sampler—A live demonstration of executive mini-amazers from this book. Includes tips on what to say and do to maximize your powers of astonishment.

Astonishing Wining and Dining—Ingenious new secrets for turning boring business lunches into unforgettable events.

Astonishing Premiums, Giveaways, and Advertising Specialties—Unique magical giveaways for clients, sales force, and customers.

Meeting Services—Individually designed tricks and illusions to communicate your message.

Call:

1-800-488-4492

or write:

Magicorp Productions, Inc.
P.O. Box 150
Wilton, Connecticut 06897-0150

Credits

Like everything else in this world, this book is a collaboration of efforts. We've borrowed a bunch of principals from a bunch of people. And therefore we would like to pay tribute to some of the original inventors. To anyone whom we have inadvertently omitted, we apologize.

We have listed the "mini-amazer" followed by the person who is most closely identified with originating the principal.

The Anytime Anywhere Legendary Book Baffler
—Al Baker and/or David Hoy

The Do-It-Yourself High-Tech Exec
—Tom Sellers

The Client Confidence Sugar Shocker
—Francis Carlyle, Ralph Hull, Marcello Trutzi

The Instant Client Dependency Syndrome
—Horace Goldin

The Just-Sign-Here Instant Approval Kit
—Edward Bag Shawe

The Tough-As-Nails Exercise Initiator
—Doc Dougherty

**The One-Too-Many-Interruptions
Ravaged Office Revenge**
—Mr. Meim

**The I-Forget-to-Do-My-Homework
Annual Report Cover-up**
—T. Anneman

**The Astonishing Executive's Official
Portable Pocket Negotiator**
—Nick Trost

The Wacky Want-Ad Business Projection
—Albert Spackman

**The Forget-Me-Not Business Card Handout #5
—Breakout Group Boredom Buster**
—Paul Curry

The Hard-to-Ignore Off-the-Wall Office Entrance
—Looy

Bill Herz

Bill Herz, founder of Magicorp Productions, Inc., entertains at over 250 corporate events a year . . . performing for executive groups from thirty to three thousand.

Bill is a graduate of Amherst College and has a master's degree in business from Cornell University. When not on the road, Bill splits his time between Connecticut and New York, always in search of new people he can educate with the use of the portable pocket negotiator.

Paul Harris

Paul Harris has authored over a dozen best selling books on magic, five videos, and a feature film. He divides his time between lecturing, performing, and creating advanced astonishment. Paul lives in the redwoods with a fax, a computer, and a dog named Blue.